TURNING POINTS

Whose
Kids
are
These?

Published by Barbour Publishing, Inc., P.O. Box 719, Uhrichsville, Ohio 44683, www.barbourbooks.com

Our mission is to publish and distribute inspirational products offering exceptional value and biblical encouragement to the masses.

 Member of the
Evangelical Christian
Publishers Association

Printed in the United States of America.

TURNING POINTS

KARON PHILLIPS GOODMAN

Whose
Kids
are
These?

REDISCOVERING LOVE AND LAUGHTER AS A
STEPMOM

BARBOUR
PUBLISHING

DEDICATION

To those generous women who contributed their stories,
and to the thousands just like them—this book is for
you and for those of us who continue our journeys.
May God go with us all.

CONTENTS

INTRODUCTION

"This is the hardest thing I've ever done."

If there isn't a stepmom's creed, perhaps that should be it.

I've yet to hear a stepmom say, "Oh, wow, this is just *too easy*! It's way better than I hoped for!" Maybe one day I'll hear that, but in the meantime, let's focus on the rest of us. We're the stepmoms with prematurely graying hair, a fixed look of bewilderment on our faces, diminishing levels of hope and confidence, and recognition for our efforts as hard to come by as a carbon copy.

If you can relate, then we have each other. And we have so much more. We have our families we're devoted to. We have our aspirations for this unexpected role we play. And we have our God, able to do anything and everything except leave us alone in our fear and confusion. He stands ready to hold us and help us, guide us and grace us in all we do, including this hardest thing of all. Let's do it together.

We're going to examine some challenges we all face, learn from experienced stepmoms who've trodden the path before us, and rediscover God's intimate care and control of everything that hurts so much right now. We're going to learn to draw on His power and wisdom, work within our role to help our families, and live the amazing life He's planned for us, no matter how complicated our schedules can be, whose weekend it is, or how many names are on the mailbox.

In our convoluted corners of the world, we'll find great peace and purpose in stepmothering as we lead others with our own integrity, generosity, stability, and grace.

Please join me here, won't you? Let's make it way better than we hoped for.

> *"I am the LORD; those who hope*
> *in me will not be disappointed."*
> ISAIAH 49:23

Chapter 1

You're Not Alone

. . .BUT IT SURE HURTS LIKE IT SOMETIMES

Make a joyful shout to the LORD, all you lands!
Serve the LORD with gladness;
Come before His presence with singing.
Know that the LORD, He is God;
It is He who has made us, and not we ourselves;
We are His people and the sheep of His pasture.
Enter into His gates with thanksgiving,
And into His courts with praise.
Be thankful to Him, and bless His name.
For the LORD is good; His mercy is everlasting,
And His truth endures to all generations.
PSALM 100 NKJV

This sisterhood we've joined can feel like the strangest club in the world. We know about it, but we don't really understand the cautions by its veteran members. There are thousands just like you and me, so we wonder—how hard can it be? How long can this blending take anyway? Good grief.

Then the membership card arrives (how'd they print that "wicked" on there already?), and all that rational thinking and all those sensible-sounding expectations throw a party to mock you—you with your positive attitude they roast over the coals along with your peace and joy. But don't worry. You can regroup and recharge at your stepdaughter's birthday party tomorrow. At her mom's house, no less! Ahh. . .the relaxation's settling in already. . . .

Okay, so maybe stepmothering isn't the fairy tale you imagined and hoped for. Maybe you're feeling as isolated as an uncharted island, and lonelier than your stepkids' mom's kind thoughts about you. I know, but you're definitely not alone. God's seen to that.

When David was in fear for his life and fleeing from King Saul, Jonathan went to him in the desert and "helped him find strength in God" (1 Samuel 23:16). Are you in the desert now? Are you tired, afraid, confused, and hurt? Please know the stepmoms before you and around you understand, sporting scars of their own and armed with wisdom they never expected. I hope you'll "find strength in God" in these words, learn and enjoy along the way, and then become a Jonathan to those stepmoms who come into your life. It's where we start. It's where we finish. And here's the in-between.

When I was a young girl, back in the Mesozoic Era before video games and e-mail, my cousins and I played outside with only discarded items from our parents and our imaginations. Yes, it was a simpler time, and one stand-by game stays with me still. I remember our pine straw houses.

We'd take the rakes with their worn handles from behind the house and get to work like we'd punched a clock. We'd survey the scattered piles of pine straw at our feet and map out the design with the detail and fussiness only young girls free in the summer could master.

Then with the confidence and excitement of award-winning architects, we'd build our houses on scraped ground of dirt and stubborn blades of grass, raking four-inch-wide and two-inch-high walls of pine straw to define our rooms. We'd negotiate for more space, arguing sometimes over our privacy (as much as a ten-year-old can have with walls made of lines), or plan big parties in the grand dimensions we'd create. Then when it was time to go in, we'd leave our house to the wind and errant dogs to design further, knowing that tomorrow we'd make a better one, satisfied and unconscious of the lessons we'd learned today.

Our pine straw houses were fluid and adjustable, able to accommodate whatever my cousins and I could imagine, no matter how much it fit or didn't fit into traditional building practices. We knew we could make it work, and every day was a new adventure.

It can be hard to think of our steplives as adventures, at least in the normally good sense of the word, when we're facing the realities of fear and insecurity, complicated schedules and tight finances, ex-wives and rejection from stepkids, hurt feelings and interrupted plans.

We may discover life as a stepmom to be inhospitable, to put it delicately—like stepping into the world's most overgrown bush of thorns with barely a rosebud to be seen. But even if that's your life now, trust that it can grow. It can change. It can bloom joy and peace and purpose, despite the doubts and no matter how many do-overs you need. You can rake those walls however you want them, into a design that houses your family in faith, hope, and trust in God, our God who will guide and sustain you through your life adventure, as you step high all the way.

THE CHOSEN UNEXPECTED

No one ever grows up saying, "I want to be a stepmom one day." We don't write "Mrs. Prince Charming and his kids" in the margins of our notebooks. We might think about swaddling a newborn, but never imagine picking up a pouting four-year-old or a sullen preteen for forty-eight hours of torture, or becoming overnight a full-time mom, welcomed or not. We can see a house full of kids in our future, but in our fantasies we never questioned their biology or thought we'd be raising kids belonging to someone else.

And yet here we are. Through redesigned dreams and repackaged plans, a new life unfolds, and we open a present we picked for ourselves to find it different from what we wrapped. Our vocabularies become directories of "child support," "visitation," and "court order." Preparing for an event means consulting someone else's calendar. Holiday celebrations develop into exercises in global diplomacy. From an "ours" baby to shared grandbabies, the adjustments keep coming, and sometimes we're overwhelmed by the horror and heaviness of it all.

There's no item on a checklist we can mark off when we add the "stepmom" task to all our others, but there's plenty that comes with it: the confusion and despair, the fatigue and exasperation, and the surprising pain and anger we never thought we'd know. Stepmotherhood sometimes brings out the worst in us, an unbecoming disposition we'd been able to hide or overcome until now.

Maybe you know that experience, when things you never thought you'd think, much less say, come out of you with the restraint of a volcano because your stepkids or their mom (or dad) do or say whatever it is that drives you mad again. Yes, we were conscious and willing when we entered into our stepfamilies, but we were unprepared. We expected much but found much more. And now our lives are full of issues we don't know how to handle, and sometimes we cry. Sometimes we think no one understands, but we're wrong.

When the hard parts of steplife are landing on us like sharp-pointed icicles broken in an earthquake, no matter how many people, friendly or otherwise, are around us, we feel alone, abandoned, isolated, empty, and defeated. It's what those before us could have told us, but we wouldn't have believed them anyway, trusting our good judgment and the "finally, everything's gonna be okay" thinking. Perhaps the struggle in all of this is one of those things we have to learn for ourselves. But we don't have to live it by ourselves.

A stepmom of six years from Nebraska has some advice for rookies, but it applies to all of us. "First, find other stepmoms to connect with on a regular basis. They are the ones who understand what it is like to be a stepmom. They will provide a listening ear, support, and understanding as you journey together. Second, remember to take time for yourself. It is important to have time each day to relax and take care of yourself. If you don't, no one else will! Your wants and needs are just as important as everyone else's. Above all, keep the faith. God has a plan for you in your new role."

OH YES, THIS ROLE, THIS UNEXPECTED ROLE

Here we are, in all our confused glory. I wish I could be with you "in real life" as the kids say, but trust that we can be together in spirit, all of us. And we can be "mutually encouraged by each other's faith" (Romans 1:12), holding one another's hand through this journey, seeking joy, discovering God more and more along the way.

Despite the surprises and sadness, the worries and wonder, the disappointments and disasters, we're not alone. We may feel forsaken, but we're very much in our Father's grasp, and He's expecting us. He has that plan we can live today, and He's ready for us.

By wisdom a house is built, and through understanding
it is established; through knowledge its rooms

are filled with rare and beautiful treasures.
PROVERBS 24:3–4

Trusting that plan means that we're going to claim and take hold of that *wisdom, understanding,* and *knowledge.* We're going to discover and help create our own *treasures.* Stepmothering is a challenge, but not one without its blessings and rewards, and it all begins with God's presence.

Like being blindfolded in an airless box, we can sometimes feel the suffocation of steplife. We begin to grasp, reach for, and desperately pursue relief, comfort, and guidance. We find ourselves with so much we don't know, and we return to the one thing we can be sure of—God's presence in the dark. Out of instinct-led self-preservation, we reach for Him, and the panicked grasp becomes a restful habit.

Our overwhelming fear turns to *wisdom,* our deep sadness becomes *understanding,* and our need for control leads to *knowledge. Treasures* from within us and throughout our families wait.

Stepmothering isn't easy, but it is revolutionary: We'll become new women as we go, stronger and wiser, making better choices every day. Let's get started.

◯ STEP STOPS

The writer of Psalm 119 wrote the longest chapter in the Bible to talk about God's Word, His presence and prescription for His followers. And in the psalmist's words, we find a crucial step for our own healing and growth.

> *The wicked are waiting to destroy me,*
> *but I will ponder your statutes.*
> PSALM 119:95

He's saying, *I may be scared and confused, but I know where to start. I'll start with my God, relying on His guidance and instruction. I'll go to His Word first and always and only then take another step.*

Perhaps our psalm writer had flesh-and-blood wicked armies or rulers after him, but let's define the *wicked* that pursues us today. Today we define it as anything that waits to destroy our peace, calm, and joy. It could be the actions of others, and we'll talk about that, but it could also be our own preconceptions, fears, assumptions, anger, insecurities, anxiety, or habits that lie in wait to pounce and plunder our hearts.

The *wicked* is anything that interferes with our building the best steplife we can. And we all know we don't need any more interruptions to our perfectly prepared plan. Well, we had a plan once, and maybe it's looking a little like a toddler's attempt at origami by now, but still, we try. And we need some guidance.

The Step Stops you'll find throughout this book are reminders and assists to help you stop, turn to God, and take a moment to gather up your plan before you deal with whatever is demanding a response. These Step Stops are designed to help you ponder God's Word, guidance, presence, and grace so that you can wisely choose how to best handle anything, no matter how wicked.

God understands our helpless and hopeless feelings, and He hasn't left us without a way to learn as we go. He'll meet us where we are every time, and prepare us well amid the fear. It's your call: Stop when the next step-crisis starts, pray, and then follow God's guidance to "let your conversation be always full of grace, seasoned with salt, so that you may know how to answer everyone" (Colossians 4:6).

◖ STEPPING STRONG

Building on our foundation in God's guidance, in each chapter you'll also find points for Stepping Strong. These are specific steps you can take to help with various issues, rooted in faith and practicality. Not every point will work for you, but here you'll find some strategies to try and ideas to consider.

In writing to the Romans, Paul wanted believers to be great examples of God's grace, to live their lives in a way that brought glory to Him and peace to them and those around them.

> *Therefore let us stop passing judgment on one another.*
> *Instead, make up your mind not to put any stumbling*
> *block or obstacle in your brother's way.*
> ROMANS 14:13

That's our job, too, to live well, to recognize that our actions impact others, and to choose stability in God and His Word over our own fears and insecurities. And we have ample opportunities to be both model for others and master of ourselves. We can't change people and circumstances, but we can change our approach to one of hope and peace. Paul says not to go forward out of vindictiveness or revenge, but to demonstrate Christ in our choices, touching others by the way we live our lives.

These suggested steps will cover some common stepmom

issues, but beyond that, they're designed to teach you how to walk with strong steps through the unique issues *you* face. We certainly don't come into this stepmom role knowing everything or even being the slightest bit prepared for what will be expected of us, but we can learn as we go. I hope the points in Stepping Strong will help you renew and fine-tune your efforts for a more joyful steplife.

JOY. REALLY?

I didn't know real fear until I became a stepmom. I didn't know real insecurity or confusion. I didn't know that one choice to pursue one path could almost destroy one daughter of God. And I didn't know that path could carry me to a kind of joy God reserves for those of us who will die without it.

It's not a joy of having all you want. It's not a joy of getting everything your way. It's not a joy of delight in someone else's heartache. It's a joy of unfolding, a joy of discovering, and a joy of overcoming. It's a joy of building a life on foundations of grace with rafters of devotion. It's a joy fought for and won where there isn't a loser, a joy redefined and reassigned to sustain me when the world threatens to take it away.

Many years ago when I was a young stepmom, joy to me was as foreign as water on Pluto. I tried to manufacture it by assembling the life I'd planned, but like paper dolls come to life, the actors in my play had the nerve to have opinions of their own and behaviors that left me anything but joyful. So I cried. I protested. I complained. I demanded. I almost didn't make it.

But God's bigger play was under way, and I was allowed all the opinions and behavior I could come up with. He'd let me cry and protest, complain and demand as loud and as long as I wanted. And He'd respond. He set about teaching me what real joy was, and how controlling myself was much sweeter than controlling the rest of the world. He replaced my hurt with His healing, taking me by the hand to walk one more day in the land where I was the foreigner.

With three boys in the house, ages seven, ten, and eleven when my husband and I married, the peaceful transition to one family I had imagined wasn't happening at the pace I expected. With our boys' other parents heavily involved in their lives, the cocoon I wanted around us looked like a scud missile target, with holes I couldn't patch despite the shingles of control I nailed down every chance I got. I had good reason. I'm sure you understand.

But if I couldn't know everything, decide everything, control everything, how could I find any joy? How could anything less than perfect be perfect enough? Our boys caught on quickly, accepting the family-of-wherever-they-were without the demands and restrictions I put on every moment of my life, grateful for the joy they created and accepted. Why would it take me so long?

I'm slow and stubborn, but you don't have to be. I know you wonder: Joy, *really*, in the hardest thing we've ever done? Yes, for you and for me.

Maybe you're skeptical. Maybe the idea of finding joy in your steplife seems ridiculous, so you laugh to keep from crying. Maybe you're ready to give up. Please don't. God is there in the hurt and the doubt, overflowing with joy for you. Walk this journey with Him at your side and in the lead. You can start now.

> *You have made known to me the path of life;*
> *you will fill me with joy in your presence.*
> PSALM 16:11

Chapter 2

Make a joyful shout to the LORD, all you lands!
PSALM 100:1 NKJV

... OKAY, I'LL SHOUT: HELP! WHAT AM I DOING HERE?

You know that dream you wake up from screaming, crying, sweating, still scared to death but oh so glad it wasn't real? That's what stepmothering can be like, just without the waking-up-relieved part. And maybe we do start shouting to God, at least on the inside, wondering how we're going to survive this turn in our lives that's much harder than we expected. We wonder how we'll ever feel at peace and in control again, considering all the people who are now part of our legal files and holidays. We work and try and smile, to start again every day, sometimes lost, always tired (but not without a good excuse for dark circles, wrinkles, and bad hair days—what a bonus, oh yeah). We pray, but does He hear our muffled cries?

Will our prayers and efforts help when we're completely out of our comfort *hemisphere*, forget *zone*? We watch the peace and joy we'd known not that long ago scatter like light from a sparkler, and we wonder some more. When the here and now gets tough and painful, when the feeling of powerlessness is stronger than hunger, when we don't know the next thing to do, we cry some more and wonder, what are we *doing* here?

Only God knows.

The parallels aren't perfect, but we can learn a lot from Jonah's story. Let's take a look. . . .

During Jonah's time, almost eight hundred years before the birth of Christ, the Assyrians to the north of Israel were an evil, pagan people, enemies of the Jewish people. God could have winked and washed them down the Dead Sea if He'd wanted, and their destruction wasn't an impossibility, but God had other plans. And He had plans for a helper.

"Go to the great city of Nineveh [the capital of Assyria] and preach against it, because its wickedness has come up before me," God said to Jonah (Jonah 1:2). But Jonah didn't want to go. Perhaps he thought the Assyrians weren't worth the trouble or weren't special enough to receive God's salvation. Perhaps he was afraid to deliver the message of God's warning or to face the wrath of an unfriendly people. Perhaps he was like we are some of the time.

Stepmoms often confide that they feel like outsiders, unrequested interlopers with no welcome wagons or warm fuzzies to lighten the load. And that load can be heavy for some stepmoms: more kids, more responsibility, and more brainpower and nerves needed to grasp this new life that feels like a new planet.

Even stepmoms with years of experience can still feel a burden unmitigated by love, affection, and respect from those closest to them. A frightful city to face? Yes, we can relate to Jonah's predicament.

Not that those around us are evil or that our safety is in question, but God has a message for us to deliver, too, just in case you thought this was all games and gummy bears. Have you discovered your message for your family yet? Do you want to? How far will you run from God to keep from living and delivering it?

Jonah took a boat trip, trying to get away from God. It didn't work. Those on the ship, panicked by the storm God sent, went to Jonah for relief.

"What should we do to you to make the sea calm down for us?" (v. 11) they wanted to know.

(Don't you imagine sometimes that those around us who might not love us so much could think the same thing? "Hmmm. . .my life would be fine if I could just get rid of her. *She's* the reason for all this calamity and destruction. . . ." Oh well, I digress; maybe that would just be my folks.)

Jonah did know that God was in pursuit of him and that's why the boat was about to sink in the storm. He told the sailors to throw him into the sea, afraid, overwhelmed, and, at that point, perhaps ready to give up and even die to escape the God-given task before him. But as we're learning more and more each day—that doesn't work. God's message demands to be lived and delivered in us all, and any attempt to outsmart Him will not succeed. He'll just work around our reckoning.

They took Jonah and threw him overboard, and the raging sea grew calm. . . . But the LORD provided a great fish to swallow Jonah, and Jonah was inside the fish three days and three nights.
JONAH 1:15, 17

Well, isn't that a pretty picture we know well. That's agreeing to leave work early to pick up your stepdaughter from play practice only to learn she left with a friend and didn't call. That's working with her mom on a schedule and making plans and preparations only to have Mom and Dad change the schedule without bothering to let you know. That's going to your stepson's baseball game only to have him behave as if you didn't exist or he just wishes you didn't.

Yeah, we know the from-the-sinking-boat-into-the-fish-belly deal. It happens all the time. These situations blow in hard like a storm, and despite our obvious distress and deep need to scream a little, the message God authored remains. Constant as the North Star, it follows us and demands the unique voice we have to deliver it. The fish belly is just a detour. Jonah figured it out fairly quickly, and God was waiting.

He wasn't going to forget about His message, and He wasn't going to find someone else to partner with in the mission. He wanted Jonah, and He wants you and me. He wants us to understand and experience the grace and joy that define Him and then to spread them to those around us whether they believe in them or not. He understands it may not be easy.

Perhaps Jonah's predicament wasn't exactly of his own choosing, and things are a bit different with us as we're living our chosen but unexpected path. But regardless of the path, here we are, sometimes wanting to run away, yet knowing the whale's belly awaits.

Being a Jonah in our families means following God's guidance and example even when we don't see His greater view of our lives. Jonah didn't want to be the bearer of God's grace to the Assyrians. He was willing to give up his own peace and joy to keep others in their own misery. But God wasn't. He saw an opportunity for healing, and He took it, even with a reluctant follower.

> *Then the word of the LORD came to Jonah a second time:*
> *"Go to the great city of Nineveh and proclaim to it*
> *the message I give you." Jonah obeyed.*
> JONAH 3:1–3

God sees an opportunity for healing in your family, too. He sees a place of pain and loss where He can grow hope and joy. Are you willing to partner with Him? How wet do you want to be?

◯ STEP STOP

God's message that comes through us will always benefit those in our family, but we must realize: the message is *about* us, too.

Before Jesus asked Peter to deliver His message to you and me, He made sure Peter lived the message in his heart. "What about you?" he asked. "Who do you say I am?" (Luke 9:20).

As we become messengers of God's grace, forgiveness, and wisdom, do we live these things as well as we tell them? As we preach trust in Him to take care of our families and guide us through these storms, do we practice it? Everything we are and everything we do answers Jesus' question: "Who do you say I am?"

◯ STILL AND TRUSTING

When I started grammar school, it wasn't pretty. I would cry like a teenager without a cell phone as my mom drove through the circle for drop-off, cling to the door handle, and beg not to be sent in. There was no reason for my fear, because it was a perfectly lovely school, with almost no witches in the closet or shackles in the cloakroom. But it was new. It was unfamiliar. It was out of my control. That's a little like steplife.

Once we're old enough, we need to go to school. Once we become stepmoms, we need to stop clinging to the door handle of our control zone and go on in to the enemy's camp—uh, sorry, I mean the new and exciting playground awaiting us. Yes, I know that can sound like a stretch, but bear with me here.

Sure, it's easy to see the other kids playing in the sandbox, swinging high, hanging from the monkey bars, and balancing on the seesaw. It's easy to feel outside their history and unwelcomed by their established alliances. It's easy to backpedal to the chain-link fence and hold on to the bar across the top, wishing for some adult supervision to level the field. Often it doesn't come.

So, feeling overwhelmed, outnumbered, horrified, and isolated, we often find it's up to us to make up the rules as we go along. It's up to us to scope out the terrain and build our own section of the jungle gym. It's up to us to supervise ourselves.

And just like in grade school, it's okay not to know everything. If you're just beginning your steplife or if you're still trying to get a handle on it after years of work, it's okay wherever you are. It's okay to go to bed some nights with no answers, no plan, no sense of what's happening, and no idea of what tomorrow will bring. It's okay because *God* knows, and He will send us work to take care of tomorrow, and then more after that.

Kids are great at taking their lives one day at a time, trusting those who should know to prepare and take care of all they can't. That's what we know of our God, and that's why you can breathe in peace, because "the LORD longs to be gracious to you; he rises to show you compassion. For the LORD is a God of justice. Blessed are all who wait for him!" (Isaiah 30:18).

May we learn to wait in trusting expectation, because it's okay to rest in "at least I know *God* knows." It's comfort in an instant, working every time.

OVERWHELMED AND UNDERPREPARED

Overwhelmed is probably the stepmom's most easily defined feeling. Too much stuff, too much chaos, too much insecurity, too much responsibility, waaaaaaaay too many people to deal with, and too many times asking yourself again, "What am I *doing* here?" Here's a little reality check for you. Those people and situations may not get a whole lot better anytime soon. But you'll get a whole lot better at dealing with it all. I promise.

So "prepare your minds for action" as Peter said (1 Peter 1:13) and believe with me as we journey through episodes we can't ever explain yet through which we come out changed. Jonah saw God's grace, compassion, and justice in a whole new way after his surf-and-turf experience. That's because God never leads us through any darkness without a sunrise and rainbow waiting for us.

In the meantime, that overwhelming feeling you know well is perfectly normal. Ask any stepmom with more than five minutes' experience. Even as prepared as we may think we are, the realitites of steplife fall on us like shotgun pellets, and they are all over and painful when they hit. We know the drill, but God didn't leave us without strategies to deal with the strange and the stressful.

Married just a few months, I remember thinking, "I used to follow fire trucks and track through pastures to marijuana fields for the story when I was a reporter. Cranky city councilmen and tight deadlines meant nothing. I was so together. . . ." Oh, the lure of false confidence.

One encounter with a surly stepchild or one phone call too many that week from his mom, and I was just about useless. Seeking shelter like a colt locked out of the barn during a storm, I retreated as far as I could without seeking witness protection and hoped my control and confidence were the only casualties to come. How could I know I'd have to lose everything to find what I needed.

God knows; He tried to help. He offered me the same instructions Jesus gave the twelve He sent out (here's my condensed version): "Do as I say, help where you can, and don't worry about the rest." He even prepared them for the less than warm reception they might receive. We can understand that scenario because we've lived it.

*"Freely you have received, freely give. . . . If anyone
will not welcome you or listen to your words, shake the
dust off your feet when you leave that home or town."*
MATTHEW 10:8, 14

Jesus' instructions were just as applicable to me, a Jonah in a ponytail and sundress, to do what He sent me out to do, to pass along His blessings, and to leave what I couldn't do to someone else. Being the stubborn, nonconformist that I am, I had a little trouble with all parts of that charge, resisting His commands, afraid to share, too stubborn to release my grip on everything within the whole family tree, too overwhelmed to make any sense of my days or my life. Don't you just know He loves the chance to, ahem, grow and develop one of His more unruly sorts?

I don't know now why it was so important that my stepsons' laundry they carried to their mom's be folded with the care of dinner napkins at the White House. I don't know now why an unexpected child on my doorstep sent me into panic that should be reserved for a smoke detector alarming at midnight. I don't know now why a conversation between my husband and the boys' mom that I couldn't hear was the equivalent of blown-away smoke signals during the French and Indian War.

And while I was hyperventilating over these clearly seismic events, Jesus was still there with His commands, waiting, empowering, preparing me more, knowing the fear that was strangling me from the inside out. It seems like it took me forever to trust myself with this promise: "You will be given what to say, for it will not be you speaking, but the Spirit of your Father speaking through you" (Matthew 10:19–20).

I was so scared, needing to say so much and afraid to say a word. And I was slow, a lot slower in following Jesus' commands than the original listeners, but He waited with me. He always does. If you're not there yet, He's waiting with you, too.

Let's look at a few strategies that will help us battle and defeat that overwhelmed feeling. Some days we do pretty well, and other days we are a train wreck, but these practices will be helpful any day and in any situation.

I can learn to look at me first. That horrible lack of control is one of the worst by-products of steplife, sort of like being swirled around in a tornado and knowing it. There's plenty of pain and blame flying around, but there's only one place to look for something stable: inside, at the core. "Let's start with you," God says. "Let's see if we can get control *there*. You need only worry about what's yours. That's enough. That's a place we can touch and work with."

Learning to look at my own behavior before I panicked because of everyone else's wasn't the most fun or quickest thing I've ever done, but it was constructive and released great burdens from me. This practice doesn't mean that we take the blame for everything or excuse everyone's hurtful words and deeds—in fact, it allows us to stop obsessing over their faults at all. It means that we look at what part we played in the situation and how we could perhaps change it or make it somewhat better by a change in our own behavior. It's a bit of control when we need it so much. Jesus gave it to us: "Listen to me, everyone, and understand this. Nothing outside a man can make him 'unclean' by going into him. Rather, it is what comes out of a man that makes him 'unclean' " (Mark 7:14–15).

Nothing the kids or Mom or the mother-in-law or anyone else says or does can change who we are. No one else's poor choices or vindictive attitudes have to become ours. Not one behavior from someone else is our responsibility—but we have plenty of responsibility for our own. And that's a charge we learn to love and depend on in even greater challenges.

Measuring our actions with Jesus' yardstick helps take away that overwhelmed feeling and replace it with empowerment. We know what the rules are for ourselves, and we can work within them just fine. That's something we can touch.

I can check my gut for fear. Just like the Israelites who were afraid when Moses was away on Mt. Sinai longer than they expected, we can react out of fear sometimes when a little logic and calm would be much more beneficial. But we know that fear very well, don't we? It can be closer than our skin, more threatening than a burglar at the door. The fear can turn us into something we're not and lead us to behaviors both destructive and long lasting. You remember the calf, don't you?

When the people saw that Moses was so long in coming down from the mountain, they gathered around Aaron and said, "Come, make

*us gods who will go before us. As for this fellow Moses who brought
us up out of Egypt, we don't know what has happened to him."*
EXODUS 32:1

The Israelites chose not to trust in their God but to build a calf-god of gold instead because they were afraid and doubtful, feeling alone and abandoned. Worried about what might happen next, about what to do, about where they'd go from there, they reacted rashly and regrettably. They built a monument to everything outside them without relying on what was within them. What have we built out of fear?

Have we built habits of suspicion, lashing out and criticizing everyone else before they can criticize us? Have we built bunkers of sadness, allowing no joy to enter because it might be interrupted anyway? Have we built walls of apathy, refusing to open ourselves up to the family we have because we don't see things getting any better?

When we react out of fear, we always have something to show for it, like the Israelites did. We'll have some big, ugly advertisement of our insecurity and lack of trust in God. Maybe we'll scream into the phone when Mom makes a hurtful comment. Maybe we'll refuse to forgive a stepchild for a bitter rejection. Maybe we'll pick a fight about Mom's request when Dad agrees too readily. While there may well be reason to discuss or deal with these situations and thousands like them, reacting in fear won't get us to that place of understanding and progress. It'll only erect a block between us and those around us when what we need is a bridge.

So before I build a calf-god, I can check my motivation. If fear is flaming the fire, I need to put it out. I can instead react out of trust, trust in God and myself to deal with a situation I might not understand any better than the Israelites did. But I can learn from their mistakes and hopefully prevent a few of my own. It's my choice.

I can just stick to the plan. Remember Jonah? He was no doubt one overwhelmed fellow. Despite his feelings and fears, God had a plan and wasn't about to alter it because Jonah was a wimp. He sorta told me the same thing, and I can't say I listened any faster than Jonah did. And while I didn't actually run away, every time I behaved in a way that didn't reflect Him, I was refusing my part in the plan I helped create.

It was my choice to help form this stepfamily. It was my choice to be another mom to my stepsons. It was my choice to forever alter my life and turn it into something I'd never imagined. So God said, "Okay, we'll work where you are. My love, grace, and guidance haven't changed. Live that."

And yet I resisted. Could those around me sense it like the sailors on the ship with Jonah? When the storm began, they knew he somehow had some responsibility in it, and Jonah first tried to escape it by sleeping.

> *The captain went to him and said, "How can you sleep?*
> *Get up and call on your god!"*
> JONAH 1:6

And that's our responsibility now. Only God can calm the storms, but we need to do our job while He does His, because the charge remains. God's telling us, "There's nothing overwhelming about delivering the message I've given you, so do that, and leave all the overwhelming stuff to Me. I can handle it."

God's message through Jonah was one of repentance and salvation, and His message through you and me is one of grace, forgiveness, compassion, humility, joy, and His request that we live it every day, stick to the plan He's made to work for our lives. I can get up and call on my God. "Don't be afraid. Focus on that plan," He tells me, "and you'll have fewer brain cells to focus on the storms." He knows me so well.

Maybe you have brainpower to spare, but not me, so He knows the less I worry about what I can't control, the more I can concentrate on what I *can* control, and that's always me and my part of where we are now. And that brings us to this final strategy.

I can set an example. If there's a place where people watch you more than in a stepfamily, particularly a fresh one, I don't know what it is. So while that's a burden slightly lighter than the moon, it's also an opportunity. And since we're on display, we may as well make it worth the price of admission.

Paul wrote to Titus so that Titus could lead and teach young Christians in Crete, where times and work were hard. He doesn't specifically mention stepfamilies among the troubled, but who knows? Paul tells Titus how to model a holy life for those watching. And God tells us.

In everything set them an example by doing what is good.
In your teaching show integrity, seriousness and
soundness of speech that cannot be condemned.
TITUS 2:7–8

I know, maybe you think that sounds too formal, too demanding, and frankly impossible. But no, God isn't asking of us anything *He* won't supply. We can only be an example to others if we have an example to follow ourselves. And that's our Father, who we discover is waiting for our shouts, seeking our trust, holding our hearts, and responding: an example as close as they come, and we learn more the closer we get.

Implementing this strategy will perhaps make the others seem easy, because to do this—to set an example—we have to know our example well, and that means knowing our God. When we know His ways, we can make them our own. When we know His grace, we can pass it on. When we know His presence, we know the peace everyone around us wants, and we can help them live it themselves.

We're not lost or abandoned or alone, and because of that, we don't have to feel overwhelmed. We can feel understood, supported, and directed, and we can reflect that better place to those around us. We can be Jonah out of the fish, newly focused and divinely calmed. And un-overwhelmed (is that a word? no matter, stepmoms understand), we can move on, with hope and faith in the good to come. A joyful shout is on its way!

STEPPING STRONG. . .WHEN THE MESSAGE IS UNWELCOME

Some stepmoms speak kindness and compassion to their families, and no one cares. Some seek to teach and mentor, but the help is refused. How do we deliver a message no one wants to hear?

1. We live it anyway. If those whom we want to touch reject us, we can live our message and let others see. Sometimes the indirect approach works well.

2. We can honor their wishes. Maybe another time will come when our message will be more welcomed, and it will still be just as valid.

3. We can seek their message. Our learning never stops, so we can listen to what others have to teach us and perhaps, through that, refine our message even more.

He who began a good work in you
will carry it on to completion.
Philippians 1:6

◔ IT'S NOT THE SEEDS' FAULT

The temptation is always there to wonder if all our work and all those tough choices (because it's rarely easy to set a good example for someone who would sell you on eBay if she thought she could get away with it) are doing any good. It's tempting to look at the high road as a lonely route to nowhere and see our efforts scattered like used litter and just as appreciated. But we have another way of looking at these strategies that makes our work easier: It helps to know it's not the seeds' fault.

When Jesus spoke to His followers by the lake in Galilee, He told them a story about a farmer who scattered seeds on various ground. Some of the seed was eaten by birds, some burned in the sun, and some was strangled by weeds. "Still other seed fell on good soil, where it produced a crop—a hundred, sixty or thirty times what was sown" (Matthew 13:8).

Put on your overalls and grab a hoe. It's our job to sow the seeds—the seeds of self-control, forgiveness, generosity, honesty, integrity, and joy—and to let God worry about what they produce. It's not our job to judge the ground, or even to tend the seeds, monitor their growth, or protect them from the elements.

And whatever happens to our seeds isn't their fault either. That's between God and those who receive them. When we sow good seeds through our words and actions, then we're out of that whale belly, setting an example Jesus gave us. And we can faithfully continue to shout to God for His help in all our seed-sowing. He'll answer every time and take care of the cultivation all by Himself.

◯ WORDS, WORDS EVERYWHERE

Sometimes we shout to God, and sometimes we just shout—loudly, angrily, and regretfully. One of the toughest areas that every stepfamily has to work through is communication: learning how to get the right messages across, keeping privacy when you need to, and overcoming the failures that lead to hurt feelings, anger, misunderstanding, and more confusion. Communicating well in a stepfamily can be tricky and tiresome, but we can learn to manage it with grace, dignity, and calm.

If we're not careful—whether new stepmoms or veterans—we'll say things we wish we hadn't, read more into someone's comment than the speaker intended, and react first and think later without knowing all the facts. If we're not careful, what we say can get us in a big mess. Let's see if we can prevent that.

Careful communication is critical, and it's also one of the first and easiest places that we can begin to "set an example by doing good." Despite all the other areas where we've lost control and all the ways we can't change the circumstances around us, we can improve our contribution to this issue immediately. There is much we can do to make the communication in our family go more smoothly.

This is a good place to begin because it's beginning at the beginning. If nothing else, we have to talk and respond to what others say every day and in every situation. And no matter the circumstance or the outcome, we will always have complete control over what we say and how we say it—and may God help us every one.

STEP STOP

It may take us awhile, years even, to master our tongues, and it's no wonder. But it's also no excuse. We can't blame anyone else for the words we spill, and only God can help us move from cleanup to prevention. Our goal is to let Him choose our words, touch them, and bless them, before they leave our lips. Our words have power to hurt or to heal, and we lose nothing in our efforts to speak love, kindness, and compassion.

Do not let any unwholesome talk come out of your mouths,
but only what is helpful for building others up according
to their needs, that it may benefit those who listen.
EPHESIANS 4:29

WHAT WE SAY

Most of us have probably said a lot of things we wish we could take back or maybe said what we needed to say in a less than kind way. (If you haven't, then trust I've done your share. You're welcome.) It's easy to speak rashly when your feelings are as raw as a carpet burn and your nerves tighter than a poet's budget. It's easy when, again, you have to defer your plans to someone else's and bend your life to accommodate someone generous with her troublemaking. But even though it's easy to be careless, it's better to be careful.

Sometimes the temptation is great. Maybe one of your stepkids mentions his mom in a favorable light, but you know something different. Or your mother-in-law criticizes the kids' mom and you want to agree. Don't. Despite how you feel about your stepkids' mom or how true what you want to say is, resist the urge to criticize her to the kids or other family members. Sure, we all need to let off some steam, and having our feelings validated by others is comforting, but what happens is that regardless of Mom's actions or comments, what's remembered is that *you* talked about it, and you become part of a scenario that you only need to view, not participate in.

> *He who guards his mouth and his tongue*
> *keeps himself from calamity.*
> PROVERBS 21:23

Stepmom Heidi's lessons are ones we can take for ourselves.

"As a stepmom, I am still learning, making mistakes, and trying to balance my family and stepfamily. The best advice that I can tell you is to try and be flexible, as hard as it may be, because if not, it will just make you bitter and feel bad, not the stepchild or their mother.

"But the *most valuable* lesson I have learned is to not discuss the stepchild's mother in front of or with the stepchild—because regardless, you are going to look like the enemy when it comes to their mother. Regardless of whether they get along or not, they are always going to take up for their mother no matter how wrong they are. I have seen this very evident with my own father, whose mother left him when he was eight. As much as she hurt him and his siblings, he was always very quick to take up for her."

Sometimes we find the confidence of good friends, online communities, or counselors, and we can say what we feel without fear of repercussion. A safe place to talk is valuable, but anyplace within your stepkids' lives isn't it. So be careful about where you talk and what you say, and remember that a couple of good responses are always available for you to give the kids and the rest of your new family.

"I don't know" is a perfectly good answer when you feel pressured into speaking ill of someone else. Even if you only repeat facts, if they're unflattering facts, you sound like someone taking too much pleasure in the situation. Stay out of it.

"I hear you" is another response you can use. Sometimes the kids may criticize their mom or repeat things they shouldn't. You can listen, comfort, and help them deal with their own feelings without volunteering your own. It takes practice and your lip may bleed for a few days, but it's a skill worth mastering.

"How can I help?" From this point, you take the "let's move on" frame of mind and encourage others to join you. These words from you move your stepkids or anyone else away from the topic that might hurt and toward healing for themselves. It's a way to not abandon the person who's hurting but instead be a positive force within the situation without adding to it. Even if there's little you can do to help (and that's often the case), your generosity and compassion stand ready.

Being the Miss Fix-Its that we stepmoms are, we often plunge in where angels don't dare intervene and smarter beings would keep their opinions as hidden as mustache bleach. We want to help, truly, but we're eager to give before others may be ready to receive. You've heard the adage that God gave us two ears and one mouth, so we should listen twice as much as we talk. Good advice, especially for a stepmom.

I know it's hard, but there's one question we need to ask, and then wait to hear the answer to, every time before we begin holding a news conference in the kitchen. The question is "Do you want my advice?" If we'll ask it generously and nonexpectantly and then listen for the "yes" before we proceed, we'll have a willing audience and the chance to genuinely offer something helpful and healing to our loved ones.

If the answer we hear is "no," then we need to respect it and accept it. Just fold up the advice you had ready, tuck it in your pocket, and save it for another day. The time will come again.

STEPPING STRONG. . .WHEN YOU'VE OVERSTEPPED YOUR BOUNDS

What about those times when your mouth gets ahead of your mind and stuff just comes out, true or not, that you'd like to take back? We don't get a rewind-and-record-over option, so we have to deal with it.

1. Apologize. The quicker the better, but if you have to wait until you see your stepchild again or talk to her mom on the phone, then wait, but don't let the incident go without an apology.

2. Explain yourself. Without taking anything away from your apology, do offer an honest explanation to the other person just for her understanding. She may not believe you or even care what prompted your behavior, but at least you'll be clear, and that's a good place to work from.

3. Know the trigger. Figure out what prompted you to react the way you did and devise a plan for handling the trigger better in the future. In most stepfamilies, difficult situations park themselves on a revolving

door, so you'll probably be facing a repeat
opportunity soon enough.

Live in peace with each other.
1 THESSALONIANS 5:13

Steplife demands lots of communication between you
and your husband, extra stuff that "normal" folks don't have
to worry about. And lots of it is private, sensitive, sometimes
painful, and uncomfortable to discuss. So when you and
your husband are talking, assume someone else could be
listening. If the kids are with you, check to see what little ears
are around the corner before the two of you discuss Mom or
money or some madness that's around you.

Did I mention that you and your husband need your
privacy? Some stepmoms have the problem of their stepkids
repeating things to Mom that are none of her—or anyone
else's—business and serve only to make difficult situations
worse. Whether they repeat what they heard correctly (which
may be damaging enough) or misunderstand and pass on
things you *didn't* say (which may take forever to straighten
out), it's a problem you can prevent. I understand that many
family matters have to be discussed with the kids and that
kids don't need to be shielded from every reality of life, but
for your own peace and privacy and sense of what little
control you have left, speak quietly and keep a watchful eye.

I know I sound like you should just wire your jaw shut
and lose a few pounds in the process of not talking too much.

I certainly don't mean that, because it's also important that we distribute information we have clearly and reliably. And sometimes it's important to keep a record.

Information in a stepfamily has a way of getting distorted, misremembered, and misused. If you have that kind of problem in your family, whether you'll ever need your documentation for court or not, keep a good record for yourself.

You may want to record information you passed along to Mom, or where you asked for information she didn't deliver. You may want to write down what you tell the kids so you don't have to deal with "Well, nobody told me. . . ." And you may want to keep a record for your husband if he's the forgetful type.

Your documentation may seem like a burden for a while, but you may come to rely on it. You have plenty to do, and arguing over what you said or what you didn't say is something you can do without. Let everyone take responsibility for acting on the information you give, and then take care of what's yours.

⊂ UNDERSTAND AND BE UNDERSTOOD

We all know the quicksand-like pile of issues just waiting to drag us down and then drop a few tree limbs full of coconuts on top of us. It's tempting to scream out in pain, blame the path that led us here and everyone with us, give up in despair, or fight for recognition of our place. One sentence will help us keep our minds on where we are and let others understand as well.

Whether in the heat of an argument, in quiet discussion, or just needing to clarify, you can always say this sentence and go from there: "This is how I feel."

That declaration puts the responsibility on you for your actions. That doesn't mean that you can justify any bad or mean behavior because you felt angry or hurt. What it means is that you claim your right to feel the way you do and the other person needs to respect that. We can't help the way we feel, but when we're honest about it, we can better deal with it and choose the best way to handle whatever's coming next.

We can't always act on our feelings either (secretly sending your stepkids' mom to a foreign country with a one-way ticket qualifies), but we can at least understand and articulate where we are and why we're struggling, and that helps the other person understand as well. Your comments may or may not change the other person's behavior (if that's something contributing to your feelings), but at least you'll have been clear in your communication. That's valuable in any relationship and especially in a stepfamily.

Likewise, your family members feel the way they feel, too, and that's the way it is. You can't change their feelings, but you can listen, understand, and withhold judgment. Whether you agree with someone's feelings or not isn't important, but you can respect them. It's a start for all of you.

⟲ STEP STOP

Why does it hurt so much? When an issue is coming between you and your husband, for example, be sure you know why you feel the way you do before you lash out or say mean things. Are you upset with Mom for something, or are you upset with Dad for siding with her? Give yourself time to think through your feelings. Stepmothering complicates those feelings, and getting control of the wild ones takes time and practice.

Be honest with yourself about what hurts the most, and then choose the best course for dealing with it.

Let the wise listen and add to their learning,
and let the discerning get guidance.
PROVERBS 1:5

(WHAT YOU SAY IN RESPONSE

Stepmothering comes with its own special set of insecurities, all wrapped up in butterfly nets easily confused with the kind used in old movies to catch crazy people. Yes, we can get a little loopy now and then, but in our defense, we're pretty good at it.

One less than flawlessly articulated, footnoted, and backed-up-in-writing comment from our stepkids, their mom, or even our husbands, and we're in need of a long, relaxing vacation. We're already questioning our own ability to handle this role, trying to monitor the words we use, and so, it's no wonder that we can quickly hear someone else's comment, take it more personally than a Pap smear, and overreact out of fear, pride, vindictiveness, or just plain lack of understanding.

This is where a shout to God is a great place to start. Go to Him with that instant scream of pain and unfairness. It's okay to carry your interpretations to Him and then listen for what to do next. Chances are, any hurtful comment was just a misspoken word or a misunderstood phrase. Either the person who hurt you didn't mean what she said or the harshness with which she said it, or you heard more than she meant.

Either way, you can respond better when you come from a position of calm and trust, calm enough to be objective, and trusting that God can see what you can't despite your best efforts. And shouting to God keeps us from shouting at others, something that will only come back on us.

Don't have anything to do with foolish and stupid arguments,
because you know they produce quarrels. And the Lord's
servant must not quarrel; instead, he must be kind
to everyone, able to teach, not resentful.
2 TIMOTHY 2:23–24

We're going to talk a lot about that servant role soon, so for now, focus on that teaching part, remembering that we're setting an example every day for our families and those who don't even want to be part of our families. It's a blessing, believe it or not.

And even if it hurts a little, consider the comments of others directed at you. Sometimes others see what we can't, and while they may be less than delicate in expressing it, we may find some truth in what they say. Perhaps not, but either way, take into consideration what others say, weigh it honestly, and if there's need for any change on your part, be strong enough to make it.

STEPPING STRONG. . .WHEN THERE'S NO TRUTH TO HER WORDS

Many a stepmom has to deal with Mom telling lies about her to the kids and others inside and outside of the family. Whether it's occasionally or all the time, stepmoms have to find a way to counter the lies without calling Mom a liar, especially to the kids. As the kids get older, they will probably see the truth for themselves, but in the meantime, when you can't ignore the lies, meet them head-on.

1. But don't overreact. Any over-the-top reaction is likely to cause more drama than the lie. Stay calm, appear unsurprised, and approach it like a math problem to be solved, not some insurmountable calculation.

2. Take the easy way first. If the lie is not terribly damaging, playing it down will usually work. Offer your stepkids a way to accept Mom and your explanation. Something nonchalant such as "I think Mom may be mistaken. . ." or "Maybe Mom didn't understand or get all the facts. . ." or "I remember something different. . ." will often be enough. These responses don't attack Mom and they give you a chance to defend yourself without sounding like a bully.

3. Move on quickly. If you're not up for any delicate discussion, dismiss the lie and move on to something else. Your stepkids may never consciously agree with you and admit their mom lied, so don't dwell on it. Give them the best of you, and let that speak for itself.

4. Don't ever give them reason to doubt you. If Mom lies, she's probably forgiven over and over. If you *ever* lie to them, you may not get another chance.

> *The LORD detests lying lips, but he delights*
> *in men who are truthful.*
> PROVERBS 12:22

When the issues we have to deal with far outnumber the happily-ever-afters we lived on before this marriage, most likely everyone, us included, will say things in less than polite and warm ways. Most likely, everyone will say some hateful things, and mean them. There may be no way around that. But *our* approach to the comments can help us deal with them more calmly and make better choices about our responses. It's a three-step process.

First, assume nothing. While it's true that most people are predictable and we can often be right in guessing what they meant, again, be sure before you react. God works on all of us all the time (that's a daily thank-you for me, I'll tell ya), so just because something's always been a certain way doesn't mean it always will be. What you assume is true may not be. Before you retaliate in word or deed, before you say something you can't take back, before you add to the problem, treat each situation as its own.

Second, ask for clarification. While you may be working hard for clarity in all your comments, others may not be so compulsive about it. When my husband asks for an aspirin, I know to offer him three different pain relievers, because even though when I say aspirin, I want aspirin, he's apt to mean any of the three options. If you know you're communicating with a fuzzy-detailer or if you're not sure, ask for clarification. Better to be a bit annoying and get the full story than to think you understand and be wrong.

Third, prepare for each response. Most situations are either/or: Either the person said something mean on purpose or he didn't, something true or false, or something critical or helpful. Decide how you'll respond in each case, answering the questions or making a decision, but always out of your own truth, dignity, and composure regardless of the other person's choices. Be ready to respond, not to retaliate. There's a big difference. Your *response* puts the focus on you and your desire to move on, wiser and stronger. Your *retaliation* puts the focus on the other person and your desire to prolong the conflict. What'll you do?

◯ STEP STOP

I know you're not one of those people whose ears salute when you hear someone whisper, "Well, I shouldn't repeat this, but she. . . ," but I'm sure you know plenty of folks who are. It's easy to get sucked into the drama and politics of a stepfamily situation, and it helps nothing.

You may hear lots of stories about your stepkids' mom from them, your in-laws, or mutual friends. You may even hear Mom tell stories about her past with the family. Sometimes those speakers will be looking for someone to validate their own thoughts or will want to involve you in the mud-raking that steplife seems to bring out in people. They usually want a response from you that matches their own. Don't do it. Let the gossip stop with you.

Though you probe my heart and examine me at night,
though you test me, you will find nothing;
I have resolved that my mouth will not sin.
PSALM 17:3

◯ WORDS APPROVED

Shouting to the Lord helps us whisper, sing, chat, talk, and shout in joy to those around us. With His guidance and preparation, we can choose our words carefully while we keep on doing our best to communicate *Him* in word and deed. We can set an example that radiates from us like the smell of bread baking, a waft of something pure.

Before we speak or speak in return to anyone in our lives, let's ask ourselves these three questions. We need a trifecta of yeses to break the silence.

> 1. Is it necessary? This is usually an opinion thing. If your comment is just about something you like or don't like that won't move the situation along, then leave it out. Focus somewhere else. Most likely everybody already knows your opinion anyway.

> 2. Is it helpful? This is usually a history thing. Going over again and again everything that's happened doesn't change it. Complaining about the past won't make you like it any better. Look for solutions, not blame.

> 3. Is it clear? This is usually just a human thing. We rattle off words like water from a

sprinkler and give no thought to where they land. But be careful, because it's always easier to defend your words if you don't have to start with "What I meant was. . ." Say what you mean and mean what you say. Maybe even write it down if you're afraid of being misunderstood. Let people know they can count on your word.

And if you can manage it, "I love you" to everyone in your house is a winner every time.

A SHOUT HE ALWAYS ANSWERS

Do you wonder if your prayers are heard, your cries noticed? Don't. Trust that Jesus is listening and waiting on you to keep up the conversation. When He was in Jericho, He was interrupted by a blind man begging. Bartimaeus "began to shout," and when the people told him to hush, he "shouted all the more" (Mark 10:47–48).

Jesus was not among those telling Bartimaeus to be quiet. He stopped specifically to listen to him more. And right now, He's doing the same for you and for me. Bartimaeus jumped to his feet and ran to Jesus. He knew that with Jesus' attention would come joy and relief.

How do we spring to our feet and run to Jesus? Do we go

to Him in expectation, in partnership, in reverence? Do we go with little hope of finding Him still waiting for us, little confidence in His interest in or ability to help us? Maybe what He's looking for in us as we shout, pray, cry, and wonder is the belief that He hears, the peace of resting in His control of our lives and simply asking in honesty for what we need. Bartimaeus had all that. And Jesus responded.

> *"What do you want me to do for you?" Jesus asked him.*
> *The blind man said, "Rabbi, I want to see." "Go," said Jesus,*
> *"your faith has healed you." Immediately he received*
> *his sight and followed Jesus along the road.*
> MARK 10:51–52

Shout all you want, ask, and believe when He says, "What do you want Me to do for you?" Ask for more faith, understanding, wisdom, and peace. Ask to be un-overwhelmed, and don't forget to ask for joy, joy, and more joy. And part of that joy comes in Bartimaeus's next choice: He followed Jesus. Looks like we're getting back a little bit of that control after all, doesn't it?

◯ JOY IN THE SILENCE AND THE SINGING

Every day we have so much to say, do, explain, question, and understand. It never ends. But we can "pause" it. We can take every opportunity to be quiet, to know God hears our thoughts and holds our fears, and to realize we don't have to explain a thing to Him because He already knows. He knows every sound of our insecurity, and He responds in chords of love. Join Him.

> *"The LORD your God is with you, he is mighty to save.*
> *He will take great delight in you, he will quiet you with*
> *his love, he will rejoice over you with singing."*
> ZEPHANIAH 3:17

Sometimes I've thought, "Hey, I've really got a handle on this stepmothering stuff, learning all about what to say and how to say it. God'll even want me to sing, too. . . ." Nah, not the way I carry a tune. I probably heard that little prompt wrong.

But God must be tone deaf. Just look.

Chapter 3

*Serve the LORD with gladness;
come before His presence with singing.*
PSALM 100:2 NKJV

. . .AND SERVE THE KIDS, AND THEIR MOM, AND THE DOG, AND THEIR MOM'S DOG, AND ALL THESE OTHER PEOPLE SUDDENLY IN MY LIFE

"Hello, my name is Stepmom, and I'll be your server for the rest of my natural life. Anything you want, don't hesitate to ask. I'm on duty for the duration. No thanks required; just hum along with me. . . ."

Do you ever feel like you may as well have said that to your family and everybody else in a nine-mile radius? Stepmothering can be a less than thankless task. In fact, it hopes one day to grow into a thankless task. While we're trying to hang on desperately to the last remaining molecules of sanity we have, we feel the demands on us multiplying like pounds after Christmas.

Incoming! This is the alarm we hear with unfortunate regularity. We reach for a hard hat, flak jacket, suit of armor, whip and chair, anything, but God says, "You don't need that; sing with Me. . . ."

I know what you're thinking—that service and singing just don't match. Let's see.

Getting your bearings in a new stepfamily or refining them in an established one takes time, patience, determination, humility, wisdom, and grace, and that's on a good day. And it's easy to feel that we negotiate from a weak position, always feeling second or third or tenth in line, as if our feelings and concerns are the last to be considered. Sadly, that's the way some stepfamilies operate because some husbands expect their wives to be instant moms to their children and the husbands' view of that role may include "everything the kids need." If that's your situation and you agree, that's fine. But if it's not, the demands and expectations Dad, Mom, in-laws, and even society in general put on a stepmom will only encourage her bitterness, resentment, distrust, and rebellion and dull her singing voice.

We need a new perspective. Whether full-time "mom," mom understudy, or mom on holidays, it doesn't matter. Our service to our family isn't about our cooking or chauffeuring—yeah, that's part of it—but our integrity and grace. And we have to hang on to both no matter how much service comes with the singing.

If the division of labor in your home is weighing heavily on your heart and back, it's time to make a few adjustments. We all need to do our part, but when one person is taken advantage of by all the others, the whole won't survive.

In the early days of Christianity, the Greek followers and the Jewish followers had a tough time bringing their worlds together. Each side was afraid it would be slighted. Sound familiar? But that's not the point here. Instead, let's look at the leaders' solution.

The distraction this time was the Greeks' worry that their widows weren't being given the food they needed. The disciples didn't leave their responsibilities to tend to the matter.

*"Choose seven men from among you who are known to
be full of the Spirit and wisdom. We will turn this responsibility
over to them and will give our attention to prayer and the ministry
of the word." This proposal pleased the whole group.*
ACTS 6:3–5

We can learn a lot from this kind of service. The leaders
(that would be you and your husband in your family) didn't
allow themselves to become distracted. They treated the group
like a family, delegating responsibilities and solving problems.

It's not good that you and your husband do everything
that has to be done in your family, and you certainly shouldn't
be left with a burden you can't lift. Learn to delegate. It's not
a power play or the handing off of stuff you don't want to
do, but a way to include every member of the family to make
things better. Even small children can have responsibilities,
and certainly as your kids and stepkids become teens and
young adults, delegating is essential.

Realize that the parents' job is to work yourselves *out* of a
job. So while you'll learn to delegate chores of course, you'll
also delegate to your kids decisions and jobs that match their
age, expecting them to organize their own school projects,
for example, to manage money (either what they've made or
what they've received as gifts), and to be responsible, trusting,
honest members of the family. That may sound like a lot to
ask from angry, ungrateful, and belligerent stepkids, but if you
don't expect it, it'll never happen. And you won't be able to do
your very important job, to "serve the Lord with gladness." It
all works together, and we're about to see how.

C STEP STOP

As you and Dad work out the distribution plan for responsibilities in your home, make the reasons clear to the kids. You and Dad are stronger together, supporting each other, so live that mutual partnership for something bigger out loud so they'll know how it works.

Give everyone time to adjust to new ways and new expectations. Just keep living and demonstrating the plan. If you assume their responsibilities for them, they'll never gain any enthusiasm of their own. Building a strong family takes everyone, and it's your and Dad's responsibility to lead, not push, the kids along. When you're hit with resistance, doubt, and panic, just stick to the plan one day at a time, one example at a time.

Be completely humble and gentle;
be patient, bearing with one another in love.
EPHESIANS 4:2

RULES, NOT PRESSURE

We serve our families best when we serve God, and that means being His trusted and responsible disciples. And *that* means taking care of what He's given us. And He's given you this family around you. It's your and Dad's responsibility to rear responsible, God-serving children. It's not your responsibility to do everything but breathe for them or to allow your own convictions to be trampled in an effort to make them happy.

Sure, we want our stepkids to be happy, but we're parents, so the primary, ever-present responsibility is to parent them, and in the routine chaos and unpredictable happenings of steplife, rules help.

Basic, fundamental, indisputable rules help everywhere. Jesus knew that.

"Love the Lord your God with all your heart and with all your soul and with all your mind. . . . Love your neighbor as yourself."
MATTHEW 22:37, 39

We serve God when we follow Jesus' rules, His basic, fundamental, and indisputable rules. And He's given them to us for our benefit, taking the pressure off us to look for some three-point flow chart with eighteen subsections for every event in our lives. Jesus' rules cover all those events, and when we have similarly efficient rules for our families, we take the pressure off everyone involved, especially the kids.

This great first step of House Rules supports so much else we want to do for our families. So while you may or may not need a rule about how many cookies to have before bedtime, telling the truth is a good rule. Whether curfew's an issue or not with your stepkids, asking before you borrow someone else's belongings is a basic rule of respect no matter what.

Your House Rules can be as basic as "Love one another" if that'll do, or as specific as when to use the telephone if you need that much detail right now. The point is to lead by example. The point is to serve and teach that service to those around you. The Rules make your job a little easier.

House Rules give the family something concrete to hang on to, something objective and nonemotional to help guide everyone through the Snaky Swamps of Blending. It's treacherous navigation sometimes, and it doesn't help that everyone has a paddle and wants to direct the boat. Wounded hearts, hurt feelings, lack of concern, and selfish motives threaten to steer the family down a strangling tributary of unforgiveness or dishonesty, but the Rules can be a stronger force when used properly. They are both rudder and buoy, to guide and protect.

In the stepfamily, it's not uncommon for each partner to think the other is too lenient with his or her own kids. And there may often be some truth to that as we do see things differently where our own children are concerned. However, that difference doesn't negate our responsibility to parent them well in a challenging life.

If you and Dad are faced with this situation, your House Rules can help. Choose to establish rules, limits, and boundaries for *all* the kids to bring some peace to your entire family. The Rules aren't about your kids or his kids or even him or you. They're about making life in the full and cranky household more pleasant and easier to manage. And that's true whether the household is part-time or full-time.

Kathy, a full-time stepmom to three kids with three of her own, understands the toll of supersized parenthood.

"My husband has three kids (16, 14, 10) and I have three kids (12, 8, 6), so they all fall into every two years apart. Part of me feels completely robbed of being able to be the 'every other weekend' stepmom that does all the fun stuff. On the other hand, I do get all of the extra time to build a relationship with the kids.

"And they are the best kids, they really are, and I am so blessed to have them in my life. Along with full-time stepmothering come the challenges of being the parent not only to the kids, but sometimes to their own mother, who is so far removed from their daily lives. I know the loyalty the kids will always have to their mother first, no matter what, and that sometimes gets to be a challenge. . . ."

We understand that challenge and continue to work to complement and not compete against the kids' loyalty to their mom. Our place may never be first in their hearts, but we can fill the place we have with what God has given us to pass along, and grow in the process. We're just beginning, again.

Stepmom Cynthia knows a valuable ingredient in stepmothering the kids we inherit. She says that parent and stepparent working together works best.

"In the beginning of the marriage, your spouse needs to know pretty much everything. My husband and I would talk daily about the kids' attitudes and our interactions. I will be forever thankful that my husband really listened to me. He wanted to understand. He didn't take the attitude that 'I was the problem.' He provided me with feedback on how to handle situations. My husband actually coached me on how to parent his children. And I listened. This is key.

"The biological parent must back up the stepparent and be the communicator in the home until firm boundaries are established. I will honestly tell you that if my husband had not listened to me and coached me, if he had not interceded for me in front of mostly his strong-willed child, it is possible we would have ended up another very sad divorce statistic.

"He also went to his kids and talked with them and set firm rules and guidelines on what was acceptable and unacceptable behavior. For every biological parent, please listen to your spouse. Most stepparents are feeling lost and uncertain. Remember the stepparent has to learn more personalities, those of the spouse and kids. The spouse and kids generally just have to learn one personality. I know there are a wide variety of family circumstances, but in my case, I had to learn to live with my husband and two young girls. They just had to learn to live with me. So there can be a lot more pressure on the stepparent."

STEPPING STRONG. . .WHEN THERE'S NO STOPPING

The full-time stepmom serves with a different mind-set, with both more and less pressure. Endurance is a necessity, and a full shot of perspective helps.

1. Focus on the positive. Stepmoms living with their stepchildren all or most of the time can parent without the interruptions part-time stepmoms face. It's generally easier to establish routines and work on goals.

2. Address issues quickly. Whether you have to so that you can move on to other things or whether you want to so that you can understand and repair damage, constant togetherness allows for more opportunity to tackle problems head-on when they occur.

3. Make long-range plans. Keenly in tune with the dynamics and intricacies of your family, you have a clear idea of where you're headed and how you want to get there. A family less separated means that making plans, adjusting those plans, and living them well is more manageable.

May the God who gives endurance and encouragement give you a spirit of unity among yourselves as you follow Christ Jesus.
ROMANS 15:5

⟲ SERVING BY THE CLOCK

I wish the courts or whoever's in charge would come up with a better word than *visitation* for time spent with the noncustodial parent. You *visit* someone in the hospital, or perhaps you *visit* your parents when you're grown up and live on your own. Children who don't live with their dad don't *visit* him and their stepmom. They live with them when they aren't living with their mom.

Granted, it may be a limited amount of time, and it may be structured by a legally imposed calendar, but it's *living* nonetheless. Think of the time kids spend with their noncustodial parent as just that: time in the home and company of the rest of their family, not the stilted and temporary image that "visitation" conjures up. And when the parents look at it the right way, kids do, too, and then they understand that House Rules apply to everybody in the family whether they're in the house every day, once a month, or once a year.

"But I'm only here a little while. . . . I don't have to do that at Mom's. . . . It's not fair!" And the wailing goes on and on. The kids who are expected to live with the House Rules during "visitation" may resent them and not be shy in saying so. But keeping your Rules isn't about forcing someone to do something or about making your life easier. It's about operating like the family you are—not the perfect, nuclear, easy-to-define family you'll never be, but the family you're becoming where everyone is valued equally. And because your and Dad's responsibility to the kids who may "visit" is no less important than it is to kids who may live with you full-time, serving God with them means teaching, modeling, and *parenting* by inclusion, not separation.

To excuse kids who "visit" from the rest of the family's responsibilities and behavior only tells them, "You're different, not like the rest of us." That kind of division makes it hard for your kids and stepkids to form meaningful and trusting relationships. Your goal isn't to draw lines, but *circles*, all-encompassing loops that bring together instead of separate.

◐ STEP STOP

None of us likes to hear something's "for our own good." Kids don't want to hear the philosophical approach you have to everybody doing their own laundry. And "because I love you" won't appease a surly teenager. But do your best to help them see that your House Rules are about love, family, and the future you're building today, the future of *everyone*.

We only fight for what matters. We only keep trying if we care about the outcome. And we only apply House Rules to everyone because everyone matters. To exclude or excuse someone means we just don't care enough. And that's not a stepmom habit.

Do everything in love.
1 CORINTHIANS 16:14

Of course, no set of rules, no matter how well-intentioned and established, will be perfect. Even the United States Constitution has amendments, so don't be afraid to revisit your House Rules or adjust the parameters. And remember that we began this discussion partly focusing on the division of labor in your home. But don't get stuck there. Don't be afraid to take on more responsibility if you want it and feel comfortable with it. Just remember that the tiniest thing we give and do out of choice is better than the biggest effort coupled with resentment.

Stepmom Cynthia understands and says we can work on

avoiding resentment toward the kids when we envision doing all we do for God.

"It's so easy to become resentful when you are driving the kids to school or functions and they completely ignore you or refuse to thank you, or you give them a gift and they totally reject it. When this happens on a daily basis, which turns into weeks, which turns into months, and in my case years, it's very hard not to take it personally and resent it.

"In my case I had to take the kids to school, and in most cases my husband picked them up. Because his oldest daughter treated me so poorly and the biological mother was behind much of this, I drew a boundary and made it clear that any extra activities would be on them, the biological parents. When I would take the kids to school, I would often pray for them both, but especially for the strong-willed girl. By setting boundaries I empowered myself without causing problems in our marriage."

When a stepmom feels pressed into a role she doesn't want and without recourse, the anger will morph into fatigue and hopelessness. Because it's hard to see beyond the next day if the "blending" isn't going well, it's easy to see calling it quits on this steplife instead. We don't want to fail, but we don't want to hurt anymore. We need the pruning shears.

> *"I am the true vine, and my Father is the gardener.*
> *He cuts off every branch in me that bears no fruit."*
> JOHN 15:1–2

Uh-oh. If the loppers are after you, too, can you imagine what they'll find? There goes my Room-Mother-of-the-Year twig (no fruit there). And next is my sewing-matching-outfits-for-me-and-my-stepdaughter branch (like that's gonna happen). Not to mention my leaves of sports trivia (doesn't basketball last fifteen months of the year?). We feel positively stripped.

So what's left? What can we do if the gardening isn't going well?

> "...while every branch that does bear fruit
> he prunes so that it will be even more fruitful."
> JOHN 15:2

Okay, so there are shared gardens of green somewhere in our weed-infested efforts. Maybe there's the breakfast on Saturday morning you can share with ease. Maybe you value the understanding, nonjudgmental talks you can have with your stepson. Maybe sometimes it's the mediator role you can play between the kids or even between the kids and Dad. Something's always growing somewhere. . . .

I remember one branch, simple but solid. My younger stepson and I went to see a movie, just the two of us. We walked into our local one-story, not-that-big mall, and I couldn't find the theater (I could barely find the food court, too, so it wasn't that surprising). He looked at me the way kids look at grown-ups sometimes and shook his head. "You don't get out much, do ya?" Now all grown up himself, he probably still thinks I'm a little lame, but we had a good time that day. And more branches grew.

Now, I'll probably not go overnight camping with my husband and boys (I want my bed at bedtime, you know), but I'm the hobo dinner queen to them all. When anything rips or tears, my sewing machine and I are their favorite things. And when the boys were young, we made teddy bears and planted flowers. And they began their mock fear of my fists— "bony" and "gnarly" were their insults of choice as they folded their own hands up and attacked the air. Probably should have disciplined them severely for that, in retrospect. . . .

They didn't get a stepmom who could cook as well as their mom. They didn't get a stepmom who knew who the X-men were. They got me, and we all had to work with that. Jesus says we work where we are: in Him.

> *"Remain in me, and I will remain in you. No branch can bear fruit by itself. . . . Apart from me you can do nothing."*
> JOHN 15:4–5

No kidding. That plan of service is making more sense all the time. Serving God with gladness is serving how we know. Serve Him and do so very much. Even sing if you want. You'll thank me that my melodies are best served quietly. But if you need a hobo dinner, I'm your girl.

◯ SINGING YOUR WAY

About midnight Paul and Silas were praying and singing
hymns to God, and the other prisoners were listening to them.
ACTS 16:25

Imprisoned and perhaps afraid, Paul and Silas could have reacted in plenty of understandable ways. But they chose to sing. They believed God's presence was wherever they were, even a place of pain and death. So they served Him the only way they could, and those around them listened.

Serve Him the way only *you* can, and those around you will listen, too.

◯ STEPPING STRONG. . .WHEN YOUR FAMILY IS LIVING IN A COLD WAR ZONE

When your family members are adjusting to life together, slowly and painfully, a bout with the plague can look less disturbing. What can you do to ease the tension?

1. Keep your faith—and let them see it.
Do something that looks permanent when
everyone else is dividing up the family silver.
Go about your plan, with whatever you can
do all by yourself, with joy and confidence.

2. Keep your integrity—no matter the temptation to point out where others have lost theirs. Regardless of the fighting or complaining, avoid giving in to any name-calling or storytelling. Anything that shoves you away from your declared position drags you over to one side or the other, and that's hard to overcome.

3. Keep a surprise in your pocket—not to excuse bad behavior but to show that life goes on and we keep trying, even after a mess, fight, or disaster. Plan ahead for these situations and know how you'll meet the kids at their level. Maybe you'll plan an afternoon of board games with little ones or rent the teenagers' favorite movies and get their favorite foods—again, not to deny issues exist, but to believe better times will come.

Let us consider how we may spur one
another on toward love and good deeds.
HEBREWS 10:24

AGAIN, THE UNEXPECTED

You may know that wonderfully fleeting feeling of having everything in control. You have your responses measured and memorized. You're ready for the appointed time to blend according to the schedule you've prepared. It's sweet that we're sometimes that naive. Oh, I shouldn't sound so cynical. Sometimes it actually works. Sometimes the ideal you saw in your head plays out for real in front of your eyes. Sometimes service is a joy and a privilege and you know what you're working for is worth the effort.

And then, sometimes it doesn't work. Someone changes the plan. Someone shows up early, or late, or not at all. Someone has an emergency, and you're left to deal with the fallout. It happens. Don't panic.

Most often stepmoms have to deal with the changes inflicted on them by their stepkids' mom when she ignores a schedule or won't work around the kids' activities. Sometimes a stepmom deals with interfering in-laws who behave more like parents than grandparents to the kids, even undermining the stepmom's or dad's relationship with them. And again, cheerfully living her life at the mercy of those around her is about as likely as discovering a diamond mine in the backyard. God says to look up.

He's asking for our trust, our trust in *Him* with it all. We don't have to trust Mom or the kids or even ourselves. We see the danger and feel the doubt, yet God says to serve with gladness, to sing and be joyful (well, everybody sings out loud but me). There must be a catch. . . .

We wonder: How can we become a family when everyone inside and outside of it keeps interfering? How can I continue to bend my life around these annoying people and their tactics? How can we move forward when we keep stumbling back? "Let's take a ride," God says. . . .

FAIR HAVENS

Doesn't that sound like a fun and descriptive name for your family? *Fair Havens* conjures up images of idyllic walks in flowering meadows, all the previously warring factions hand in hand in perfect harmony, doesn't it? And that's not you? Well, what are you waiting for? Allllll *aboard*!

Alarmed at Paul's preaching, angry Jews wanted him arrested, even killed. In Jerusalem Paul requested to be tried in Rome, and since that was his right as a Roman citizen, King Agrippa had Paul loaded onto a merchant ship headed to Rome. Like a stepfamily struggling to fight winds and waves it can't control, Paul and his shipmates were facing an uncertain future.

He says they "moved along the coast with difficulty and came to a place called Fair Havens" (Acts 27:8). It was to be a stopover, just the beginning. Sometimes that's what happens to us. Things go well enough, maybe we even overcome a rough start, and we, like Paul, would like to remain there where it feels stable and safe. But it's not the best place, and others and the circumstances push us on.

Paul's ship sailed calmly for a while, but "before very long, a wind of hurricane force, called the 'northeaster,' swept down from the island" (v. 14). You may know that kind of development. Like a force of nature, it feels impossible to stop, and perhaps much of the time it is. Families of all types endure growing pains, suffer damage, and have to wade through the debris left behind so that they can ride high. We do our best to deal with the storms and learn as we go.

The sailors were afraid, so they tried to secure the boat, but that wasn't enough. Paul says, "We took such a violent battering from the storm that the next day they began to throw the cargo overboard" (v. 18).

That's a good idea, and we can do the same. The sailors threw away everything that didn't matter. I've had a few pallets of that kind of stuff myself, stashed away under the deck, riddled with mildew, and overrun with rats. How about you? Do you have any jealousy, fear, insecurity, or pride? Is the need to be right every time weighing too heavily on you?

Maybe we think all those concerns are important during calm waters, when we can manage them pretty well without too much danger. But then the storms come and turn everything upside down, exposing all we'd hoarded and didn't need. And we begin to worry. Paul was already past there, on to a sad place.

"When neither sun nor stars appeared for many days and the storm continued raging, we finally gave up all hope of being saved" (v. 20). Well, we've been there, too, haven't we? When the storm continues, we can't see past the clouds. We begin to wonder if the sun still lives. Hope fades with the confidence we loaded onto the ship of our expectations, and sailing on seems pointless.

How many times have you had that conversation with yourself? How many times have you wanted to turn back the ship and sail to more hospitable harbors? How many times have you thought that whatever happens next, no matter how bad, it can't hurt as deeply as it does now? How many times could you see only disbelief, fear, and hopelessness through the holes in your heart? But hope only fails when it's abandoned. Paul says to keep going.

"I urge you to keep up your courage, because not one of you will be lost; only the ship will be destroyed" (v. 22). Things will change, he tells the crew, but you won't be defeated. That's a good message for us. Things in our lives will definitely change, some of our own choosing and some not. How well we manage those changes and how well we keep up our courage will have much to do with the remainder of our voyage.

Despite their courage and efforts, no God-sized life jacket was about to appear in the ocean and save Paul and the sailors. They would have to work through the effects of high winds and rough seas. "Nevertheless, we must run aground on some island" (v. 26), Paul reports. Oh, a shipwreck. Now that's something we can relate to.

Sometimes we can see them coming, on the horizon, the wind getting stronger. Maybe you know the storms of a summer with a stepchild you rarely see, one who doesn't want you there when she disembarks. Maybe you know the recurring storm of a stepchild so hurt that you can't reach him and the stress it washes over your marriage. Sometimes we're knocked down by a wave we never expected, maybe the kind that shipwrecked Stepmom Cynthia. She went from favorite to hated in the time it takes to say, "I do."

"In our case, the older daughter (Lori) was nine years old and the younger daughter (Mindy) was seven. The older daughter has very strong opinions about what she likes and dislikes, and if you're on her list of dislikes, beware.

"For the first two years of our marriage, Lori completely ignored me. She wouldn't say hello, good-bye, please, or thank you. She wouldn't look at me. She refused to listen to me. She walked by me like I didn't exist. She constantly gave me dirty looks and made funny faces at me. She turned her younger sister against me.

"This may seem like just childish behavior and pranks, but believe me, when it's aimed at you. . .day after day. . .week after week. . .year after year. . .it is heartbreaking. It's hard not to take it out on your own spouse, the child's biological parent that you willingly married.

"Mindy was very sweet and loving by nature. She was

accepting and very attached to me. Mindy hugged me and gave me kisses. She listened to what I had to say. She was sweet and compliant. She simply adored me. I loved that girl like my own.

"Lori managed to turn Mindy on me for approximately six to nine months. So now I had two young girls who didn't listen to me, ignored me, were very rude and disrespectful to me, and just generally made me feel like I was the outsider and didn't belong in what they thought was their home.

"It was so bad that Lori got hold of our wedding album and attempted to destroy a photo. Thankfully, we discovered this before any true damage was done. But can you imagine being a new bride, in her new marriage, in her new home, and discovering that your wedding album, which you just received from the very expensive photographer, has been tampered with? I felt very unloved and rejected.

"I'm sure you are wondering why I married into this mess, but here's the very big secret that most stepparents don't know. Before the wedding, you are on a pedestal. These girls fought over who was going to sit with me. They used to call me 'Miss Cynthia.' They wanted to dress like me, put on their make up (pretend make up) like me. They noticed everything. They knew what kind of food I liked, how I liked to dress, what I liked to do. They adored my dog, Simba, and they got on the phone when their daddy called me and begged me to come over for dinner. They wanted me to tuck them into bed, and they wanted hugs and kisses. They listened to me. They let me bathe them and brush their hair. They were simply adorable, and they adored me. Mindy even got a Barbie doll with red hair just like 'Miss Cynthia.'

"So can you imagine getting married and coming home from the honeymoon, and pretty much overnight both of these girls are complete enemies, and I'm the one they hate? I felt devastated. I felt rejected. I felt abandoned. I felt completely overwhelmed and I wondered, how would I survive the next ten or so years and still remain married and sane?"

That's the kind of storm that scares all of us, because if we haven't experienced it, we're afraid we will. The platform we stand on can feel shakier than a bird's nest at a hundred knots. Whatever the storm, we need our strength. Paul told the sailors to eat and sustain themselves because they'd been in "constant suspense" (v. 33).

Our strength needs replenishing every moment, too, and we do that with our constant reaching for God. Like a lifeboat in the deep sea, He holds us secure while we kick our way to safety. We learn and adapt and change and find strength in our new skills at stepmothering—skills most unexpected but greatly valued.

And that adapting skill is used nearly every day. Seeing the danger in an unfamiliar place, the sailors came up with a plan to get out of the storm. But it didn't work.

When daylight came, they did not recognize the land,
but they saw a bay with a sandy beach, where they decided
to run the ship aground if they could. Cutting loose the anchors,

*they left them in the sea and at the same time untied the ropes
that held the rudders. Then they hoisted the foresail to the
wind and made for the beach. But the ship struck a sandbar
and ran aground. The bow stuck fast and would not move,
and the stern was broken to pieces by the pounding of the surf.*
ACTS 27:39–41

That's an effect we know well, too. We know how it is
when what we plan for and what we get are two different
shipwrecks. Constant practice with that situation is what
makes stepmoms so good at contingency planning. We learn
to work around schedules we don't control, to handle a fickle
stepchild's attitude that can range from agreeable to antisocial
in a blink, and to deal with Dad's erratic response to the kids'
behavior. And despite the tricky paths and troubled people
along the way, we can arrive safely.

After Paul's shipwreck, he and the other prisoners could
have been shot so they couldn't escape. But the official in
charge, the centurion, "ordered those who could swim to
jump overboard first and get to land. The rest were to get
there on planks or on pieces of the ship. In this way everyone
reached land in safety" (vv. 43–44). Perhaps the journey
wasn't pretty, but they were successful.

There may well be photos in our mind from a hard
history that we'd like to blur out or lose in a throwaway shoe
box. That's okay. Steplife is about enjoying the good when we
find it and leaving the bad behind. Blessings abound in the
oddest places.

Paul and the sailors wound up on an island called Malta. Apparently a warm reception wasn't what they expected. "The islanders showed us unusual kindness. They built a fire and welcomed us all because it was raining and cold" (Acts 28:2). Sometimes we're surprised, too, by the people in our steplife, when they welcome us in out of the rain and cold with compassion and understanding. Often we're given that opportunity—to be the hand that reaches out only to give. Our location may be a wreck, but the rainbows promise fair weather among us.

Paul's ship didn't set out for Malta, but that's where it ran aground, and Paul wasn't afraid. Instead, he healed those who were sick and was honored and trusted by the natives. He wasn't where he planned to be, but he served God with joy and singing despite the circumstances that got him there.

So if you haven't gotten to where you're going yet, serve where you are, because that's where God is. He's making a way for you to touch, love, give, and grow, so that you only move on to better places with your family. When we work where we are, we're nourished to go on.

Paul and the sailors spent three months in Malta, and their time and efforts were not wasted. An unexpected detour made their future travel easier.

They honored us in many ways and when we were ready to sail,
they furnished us with the supplies we needed.
ACTS 28:10

God's presence is wherever we are. His control of place and people and time and circumstance never fails. Land, ho!

> *Hear, O LORD, and answer me, for I am poor and needy. Guard my life, for I am devoted to you. You are my God; save your servant who trusts in you. Have mercy on me, O Lord, for I call to you all day long. Bring joy to your servant, for to you, O Lord, I lift up my soul.*
> PSALM 86:1–4

Chapter 4

*Know that the L*ORD*, He is God;*
it is He who has made us, and not we ourselves.
PSALM 100:3 NKJV

C ...YEAH, BUT HAVE YOU MET MY STEPKIDS, OR BETTER YET, THEIR MOM?

I know why the negotiators—for hostages, oil fields, lawsuits, mineral rights, anything—make the big bucks. It's tough being in the middle. And being in the middle and on the outside of a stepfamily at the same time is just about the most fun you can have on a sunny day. Who was the crazy person who said things would calm down when everybody's mail came to the same address? Oh yeah, that could have been me—or you.

But even if the boxes have been unpacked and the fight for closet space has long been over, that delightful *blending* we were told about is going more like a hostile takeover. Lord only knows what we're supposed to do now.

Well, actually, He does. He was there when we were full of hope and there when we felt it draining away. He's here now, when the nuts and bolts are falling off our carefully constructed ideal, and He knows how to help. Thank God He's got a plan that won't fall apart.

When sick people followed Jesus, He healed them. Then when they were hungry, He made sure they had something to eat. The disciples pointed out the shallow supplies, but Jesus wasn't alarmed.

"Bring them here to me," he said (Matthew 14:18), and the bounty was more than enough. He says the same to us.

He sees what we lack in this heavy role, but He's more

concerned about what we have. He surveys the situation and directs our next steps when kids and chaos reign. "Bring them here to Me," He says to us. And we learn how.

PERSONALITY PLUS OR MINUS

Sometimes I hear stories of stepmoms who enjoy the company of their stepkids, and sometimes I hear stories of stepmoms who'd rather be in a different time zone than their stepkids. Despite our best intentions, we can't make ourselves like the kids who belong to the man we love. Maybe the kids are just different from us, interested in different things, or hard to get to know. Maybe they're resentful and manipulative and don't want to like us. Regardless of their inclination, ours needs a mature route. "Bring them here to Me," He says. . . .

Stepmoms often begin their families thinking "bonding" with their new children can't be that hard. Maybe they develop a friendship before becoming a family and believe that will make the transition even smoother. And sometimes it does. Sometimes, though, kids who welcomed the new lady in Dad's life before she became "Stepmom" can rebel at the thought of another parent. And that rebellion can be long-lived.

"After the marriage actually happens and you move in with your husband and live together as a couple and head of the household, one or more or all of the kids may turn on you, the stepparent. You have become The Enemy," Stepmom Cynthia says, knowing well what it's like to live with a child who could go from huggable to horrific in a day and used her influence over her younger sister to make Cynthia's journey long and hard. But she hasn't given up.

"I'll be honest. There have been many tears, several bouts of anger, ugly moments, and nights full of regret and pain. And there's been much time in prayer and pleading to God. I'm seven years into this journey, and although the journey's still happening, I can clearly tell you that there is tremendous hope for a positive outcome."

When the bonding is more like bondage, it's then that stepmoms get to do that thing they will no doubt become famous for in some distant time and place—they love anyway. That's when we love our stepkids even if we don't like them and they don't like us. That's when we love them with the purest form of care that says, "I want what's best for you, and I'll do what I can to get it, even if you don't want me to." That's when we love them because Dad loves them and we'll wait, pray, and see if something good grows.

Stepmom Kristi's wait was relatively short.

"My husband and I were about to get married, and I was just not clicking with anyone at all! There was friction between my husband and me when we had visitation with the kids, friction between me and our son and daughter (who were about eight and five at the time), and I was seriously wondering what I had gotten myself into. I remember begging God to please give me the heart of a mother so that I could love these children the way they needed and deserved to be loved by me, so that I could be the wife and stepmom that my family needed me to be.

"God answered me in the most magnificent way. I began to give my heart to the kids, and in return, our relationship began to grow and flourish! We stopped being wary of each other and trying to guard our hearts, and we just began to love each other.

"One word of caution: In praying for the heart of a mother, my youngest son was born almost nine months to the day of our wedding. Not only did God bless me with the heart of a mother, but he blessed our family with another child!"

That love you give your stepkids won't always be returned the way Kristi's was, but you can give it anyway. It doesn't require you to share your stepdaughter's taste in music or understand your stepson's obsession with video games. It only requires you to think of them with the heart of a parent. It may take practice and even feel awkward, but it's never wrong.

When Paul began his ministry, it was new, different, and often met with resistance. The Savior's love and grace for Gentiles, too? How could it be, the early Jewish Christians wanted to know. Under arrest for his radical teaching, Paul asked to address the crowd so upset with him, but he didn't use the scholarly and more prevalent Greek.

When they heard him speak to them in Aramaic,
they became very quiet.
ACTS 22:2

Using the everyday language of the people got their attention. It showed Paul's respect for them and his eagerness to establish a common ground on which they could build a better, more inclusive future. You may feel that you and your stepkids speak completely different languages and that no one is eager to learn the other's. But perhaps they, too, are wary of something new and different—you. Perhaps bigger chasms can be crossed when we cross little ones at their level.

We stepmoms do a lot of the bending in the early stages of bonding, and this kind of effort is just another strategy we can use to usher along good results. It helps to meet the kids where they are, to speak their language. If your stepkids are into practical jokes and silliness, join them. If they're more cerebral, you can be, too. No, you can't become someone you're not, but you can enjoy the kids for who *they* are. And in those shared moments, something may begin to grow.

Lynn, a grown stepchild, remembers her stepmom very well. She remembers her with love, grace, and gratitude. May we all be so fortunate. This is her story.

"My dad's fourth wife was, I guess, my stepmom, and she was one of God's greatest gifts to me. She loved, respected, supported, and enjoyed me, way more than my mother or father ever did.

"There were many reasons my parents got divorced

(mental illness, alcoholism, vicious tempers), but somehow Betty was the blessing I received from the aftermath. She never tried to take anyone else's place in my life. She just shared her zest for living with me without limit.

"Betty had always wanted to talk to or meet my mother and tell her what a beautiful job she had done raising me (a kindly thought, as my mom was a pretty awful example most of the time). My mom was so jealous. She never once would speak to Betty, even at my wedding, even though I pleaded with her.

"Betty never took offense, and never ever took it out on me. Honestly, I would have been lost without her. She never had kids, but she treated me like her own, and I am so much more like her today than either of my parents.

"There you have it from a grown stepkid with an unusual perspective and nothing but love and appreciation and respect for a stepmom who gave me—guess what—nothing but love and appreciation and respect."

Other stepkids may take years to see what Lynn saw right away. Heidi's stepson is her husband's stepson he's raised since the age of one. Together, Heidi and her husband saw the grown man turn to God in their living room. Today he's a dad, too.

"It has taken him having a family of his own to realize how much my husband and I have done for him. His wife sent us a thank-you card to say just how much they appreciate us for being part of their family, for *still* being a part of their family. Just receiving that little thank-you card meant so much to my husband and me."

And the circle grows wider.

WHEN IT DOESN'T WORK

Paul spoke the language of the Jews. He took nothing away from their heritage. He wanted to enrich their lives, not limit them, but they were still resistant, afraid, and untrusting. Sometimes we get the same response. Sometimes we do our best, threaten no one, offer more—and still we face kids resistant, afraid, and untrusting. The rejection calls for a five-step approach:

1. Take a deep breath. It's probably not personal. To the kids, you may just be in the wrong place at the wrong time—a perceived threat to their control. Time, prayer, and circumstance will work together to shorten the gap between you.

2. Remember your communication skills. Hurt and maybe angry, you may find it easy to become defensive, combative, or insensitive with your words. It's easy to respond in ways

you'll regret later. No matter the responses of your stepkids, watch yours. Be clear, compassionate, and constantly mindful of the power of your words. Seek to understand before you explain.

3. Pay attention to their safety and well-being first. There'll be plenty of time for sorting out their feelings and yours, but you're in a position of authority (whether the kids like it or not), and that comes with the responsibility of looking out for them. Don't let that slide because your feelings are hurt. Do your job.

4. Consider a delayed reaction. Maybe you can get some help before you deal with the behavior. Maybe a different perspective from Dad, who knows them better, will help. A strategic delay may prevent an overreaction. Even if you only have a few minutes before you have to respond, use that time to pray, calm yourself, and hold on to your trust in God's control.

5. Learn and remember for the next encounter. Pay attention to your behavior as well as the kids' and let it be a lesson to you.

What worked? What didn't? What skills do you need to improve? Prepare so that you can help reduce the frequency and frustration of any rejection to come.

◠ STEP STOP

So many decisions to make, so many ways to fail—this is a stepmom's lament. Every day can be a struggle, full of new choices and risky situations. God has made us ready for all of those, too.

When he saw a woman who had been crippled for eighteen years, Jesus "called her forward and said to her, 'Woman, you are set free from your infirmity.' Then he put his hands on her, and immediately she straightened up and praised God" (Luke 13:12–13).

Then Jesus had to defend His actions to the synagogue ruler, who said that healing shouldn't take place on the Sabbath. When the opportunity appears for healing, for growth, for understanding, for insight, or for any kind of progress—let's take it. Let's risk the outcome to put our hands on whatever's wrong and try to make it right. Let's listen with reverence, serve with gladness, step with confidence, and praise with regularity. Let's remember, there's no wrong time to do the right thing.

◗ WHAT ABOUT NOW?

Along the Sea of Galilee, Jesus encountered more people who needed His healing, including a man without speech or hearing. That was about to change. With a touch and a word, "the man's ears were opened, his tongue was loosened and he began to speak plainly" (Mark 7:35). Naturally, the witnesses were amazed.

> *"He even makes the deaf hear*
> *and the mute speak."*
> MARK 7:37

Yeah, but will He make my stepkids put their trash in a trash can, or help their mom grasp the meaning of the word *compromise*? Sometimes we see the God of our universe and our heart move heaven and earth to accomplish great things. How much trouble could it be to grant us a night of pleasant dinner-table conversation or a stepchild's "thank you"?

I know, He's wondering, looking at me, "How hard could it be for *you* to listen before you judge your husband's handling of that situation with his son? How hard could it be for you to accommodate the schedule change without all that wailing and moaning? Shall I go on?"

Okay, I get it. Help *me* hear, help *me* speak, help *me* learn. I remember You made us all, and that includes me, a work in progress.

My husband and I had an argument many years into our

marriage. It was stupid. He got mad at me for absolutely no reason (you know how they do that) and then had the nerve to say, "Well, you'd be mad for a week if I'd done that!" And he was right, once upon a time. But I really had grown up and learned to handle those kinds of situations better, and it hurt me that he hadn't noticed. I was making progress, a lot of it, but instead of thinking of how much more mature I was now, he was judging me by my old behavior.

And in his defense, it was pretty bad. I can admit it. Don't want to, but I can. I'd been known to stay mad for a lot longer than a week for much less severe offenses than the one we were haggling over. And I was good at it. But it wasn't getting me anywhere. It didn't stop eruptions between two strong-willed and always-right people who had to live together. It only made the days after the eruptions more painful. So I learned.

I got better at listening, better at speaking, and *lots* better at letting go and moving on. I learned to dissect and obsess less (well, a little less) and remind myself of the good, true, and blessed things in my life more. I saw the time I was wasting and made better choices.

Maybe you've learned something new, too. Maybe you've changed and grown, getting better equipped every day for the unique challenges of your steplife. We don't have to stay "deaf" and "mute." We can let Jesus' healing amaze those around us, too. . .even if it takes some of them awhile to notice.

STEPPING STRONG. . .WHEN THE LEARNING GETS TOUGH

Experience is great, and we know that setbacks teach us well, but good grief, don't we ever learn enough? That's how it feels sometimes, doesn't it? We're doing our best and then—whack!—something lands hard on us and failure threatens to take away our progress. We panic. And if there's nobody around to beat up on us, we'll do it ourselves. Let's choose something else:

1. Replace that wringing of hands and gnashing of teeth that screams "If only. . ." with the steady breath and calm confidence of "Next time. . ." Look at each experience, mistake, or disaster not as a blunt landing from a high cliff but as a wide bridge to an open place where "next time" you'll make better choices.

2. Tell those who may not have noticed what you've learned and ask for accountability, especially with your husband. Those closest to us often have the hardest time seeing our slow but steady progress, but when we make our continuing efforts part of the landscape, they see what we sow.

3. Ask for specific healing and tell Jesus your hardest lesson to learn. Ask for opportunities to learn and polish the skills you need and put them to work. Don't run from a pop quiz or a hard test. Rely on what you know; learn what you don't. The healing comes in our willingness to let Jesus control the circumstance.

> *If anyone is in Christ, he is a new creation;*
> *the old has gone, the new has come!*
> 2 CORINTHIANS 5:17

⟲ DRAWING LINES

Bonding or breaking, the beat goes on. And even when we *are* the brilliant parents we know we can be for the kids under our roof and expect the newspaper to be calling any day for a feature story, we have to remember their other parents want a say in that, too. Oh. And it's not pretty when those parenting styles clash worse than my twenty-year-old wardrobe.

It's not uncommon for Stepmom and Dad to have a completely different way of parenting than Mom does. But guess what? It doesn't matter. She's still their mom, and whether she's a model parent or needs to be reported to the authorities, you can't control what happens outside your home. You can't make Mom's rules match yours. You can't force her to parent the way you do.

Ideally, your stepkids' mom puts them first and keeps them safe and well and provides for their needs when they're in her care. Ideally, the only differences you have to deal with are minor and don't put the kids in danger or expose them to elements you and Dad don't. And ideally, the rules for Mom's house will be close enough to the rules for your house so that the kids have a great deal of stability and continuity.

But if your life isn't the ideal, you still have to deal with it. That calls for consistent parenting from you and Dad.

No matter what the age of your stepkids or what the situation is with their mom, saying anything unkind about their mom will never be a good choice. When you and Dad are hit with "Well, Mom says it's okay" or "Mom lets us do this" or "Mom doesn't make me. . ." the only approach is *"Yes, but. . ."*

"*Yes*, we acknowledge Mom's place, Mom's rules, and Mom's choices, *but* our place, our rules, and our choices remain." The kids may not like it, they may have a fit and complain, but they won't be confused if you're clear and consistent about your parenting.

Even if the kids are only with you a small amount of time, sacrificing your better judgment just to make the immediate life "easier" or to be more popular with the kids is a bad move. Any temporary "gain" will accumulate into a stubborn pile of regrets hard to lose.

And if Mom's troublemaking is aimed at you, don't play along. Separate yourself from the fray and reduce the stress and disruption of your days. That's what Stepmom Cynthia had to do.

"In the beginning I communicated with [the kids'] mom about gifts, holidays, and schedules. Once again, before we were married, the ex-spouse was fine. But after our marriage, I believe she saw me as some kind of a threat. I'm not sure where her insecurities stemmed from, but there was a clear change.

"She tried to stir up trouble between my husband and me. She tried to allude to secrets she kept about my husband that I would eventually find out. She talked poorly about my husband and me. She criticized our every move. She criticized our home, our ways of discipline, our joint celebrations, etc.

"After approximately three or so years of her bad-mouthing and Lori's rebellious behavior toward her father and me, I gave up on trying to get along with the ex-spouse. I stopped attending most games and other functions. I stopped planning joint functions for the kids. I stopped riding with my husband to drop off or pick up the kids. I stopped answering the phone when she called, thanks to caller ID.

"When the ex-spouse picked up the kids at our home, I had them ready and at the door with their belongings and quickly had them run out to meet their mom while I quickly waved a bye and shut the door. In other words, I shut her out of my life.

"She had actually tried to turn me on my own husband. I knew whose team I was on, and it was clearly not her team. You may think these tactics a little harsh, but with the kind of person I had to deal with, it was necessary. When I stopped allowing her to be a part of my life, it stopped some of the problems my husband and I experienced.

"First of all, we shut down her opportunity to get between us. Dan became the only point of contact, and she didn't want to talk to him. Conversations were less often and brief. The drop-offs, which used to take a half hour, went down to less than five minutes. Things greatly improved.

"As a woman I intuitively saw what she was doing. She was trying to interfere in our marriage. I can remember many times telling her that she needed to discuss this or that with

Dan—that it was between the two of them. She refused to listen and kept trying to get me to influence my husband about different things. So I had no choice. I felt like I married Dan; I didn't marry the ex-spouse or the kids. Although I had agreed to help raise the kids, I didn't need to communicate with their mom unless it was an emergency."

Of course, having to draw deep lines between the kids' households isn't the most pleasant development for the kids, but in certain circumstances, it may be necessary. And if reducing your interaction with Mom allows you more peace and control over your home, you'll be better able to enjoy your role and your stepkids, too.

If staying in separate corners of a boxing ring is what your life with Mom is like, just remain open to the chance for better relations, because people, their motivations, and choices can change. The day may come when the lines drawn between your homes can blur and fade as everybody grows, gives, and forgives through the years.

⟳ LINES INSIDE

What if it's you and Dad whose parenting styles are in conflict? Yep, it happens a lot. Even parents of the same kids don't agree all the time, so it's no wonder that instant families struggle sometimes, too, especially since there's an inherently unbalanced division of power. But being "just the stepmom" doesn't mean we don't get any say in what goes on. And sometimes, it means it's okay if you don't want one.

You can probably relate to Cynthia's vivid memory.

"I can remember this moment so clearly that it could have happened only an hour ago. As I stood at the top of the stairs in my new home with my new husband, I listened to the screams, the screams of a nine-year-old girl who simply refused to listen to anything her father (my husband) had to say. Every suggestion was met with resistance.

" 'Put your shoes on,' he voiced.

" 'No!' she screamed.

" 'Where's your uniform?' he asked.

" 'I don't know,' she stubbornly blurted out.

"He made several more attempts.

"Another morning, and yet another struggle to get her off to school. After several weeks and months of this behavior, I actually had a pivotal moment at the top of the stairs. I debated whether to go in and try to help, but I had done that before and it only escalated the situation. But my pivotal thought was, 'I understand why stepparents leave.

I understand why divorce the second time around is so common.'

"I actually thought about divorce. Not for me. Not for Dan. But I had a newfound empathy for those who had gone down that road. Here I was a reasonably mature Christian woman. I was the independent type who wanted to delay marriage and children until after I finished college and was making a good living in the corporate world. And I did just that.

"I met my husband at the ripe age of forty. We courted for one year, and we were engaged for another before we married. Now I stood at the top of the stairs and could clearly empathize with all the stepparents who had left marriages because of unruly children."

It's often easy for stepmoms, having a bit of an objective outlook not clouded by time and biology, to see any trouble Dad's having parenting the kids. It's easy for stepdads to do the same thing. And when the biological parent and the stepparent are poles apart on parenting issues such as discipline, responsibility, and money, chaos in the house is a polite way to describe the inevitable fallout.

So compromise is necessary here, too. Maybe Dad's not as concerned with neatness as you are, so you focus on what might be considered health and fire code violations and let the rest go. Maybe Dad wants to pay the kids for chores and you believe everyone working together is an important part of strengthening the family. So you keep quiet about the pocket change and encourage the kids to partner with you in making other contributions to the family and home.

When the issues go beyond something minor and you and Dad have to make a decision about how to proceed, tread lightly. Don't overact. Speak softly and refuse to argue with Dad about his actions in front of the kids. It won't end well.

Then when the two of you are alone, resist the urge to say, "If *my* kids did such and such. . ." or "I would *never* do. . ." or "You're just *wrong*." Yes, you're a caring stepmom and your efforts for the family mean that your opinion matters, but you can handle these confrontations with grace and dignity.

Replace those hurtful phrases with "Have you considered . . . ?" or "Another idea would be. . ." or "What if you do this and then. . . ?"

If the current situation is a repeat event, remind Dad of the history and offer alternatives to whatever didn't work last time. Remember, if you've learned anything, be generous and pass it on. If there's new information this time, make sure that's clear. Try to keep a long-range perspective while helping Dad weigh all the factors that need to be considered for a decision.

Then something has to give. Cooperative parenting needs to be about working together toward a solution that leads the kids toward their own growth and maturity. What if you and your husband disagree on the severity of something his child has done? And what if you see more problems to come if he doesn't agree with you? What if the two of you really don't see the other's view but you have to be able to move on? Well, we can call it a great opportunity for growth. Gee, thanks.

I know this feeling. I just about had a coronary over something my husband thought was relatively minor. Don't you wish you'd been at my kitchen table that day? We discussed it calmly, but we still couldn't agree. That's where Stepmom gets to exercise those trust muscles big-time. Oh boy.

I wasn't going to let this issue become some defining moment between us. It wasn't *that* severe. So I told him to do what he wanted and I'd respect his decision. I'd told him what I thought, he'd listened, and I'd listened to him. There wasn't any need to argue about it or obsess over it. It was time to trust him to be a parent and time to trust us to be okay no matter what, by trusting God to be there in it all. It's not easy. Exercise never is.

STEP STOP

Getting to that place of trust takes time, commitment, and the abundant grace of God. He's there to meet us when we fail and to steady us as we try again. You can practice every day, with issues big or small—it doesn't matter.

Believe God's hand is on all that worries you, and trust Him to manage it and the other people involved to His glory.

Trust that He knows best when you know next to nothing. Do your part. Trust Him to do His.

God will keep in perfect peace those whose minds are steadfast, because they trust in Him.

> *Trust in the LORD forever, for the LORD,*
> *the LORD, is the Rock eternal.*
> ISAIAH 26:4

What if there's no question about your stepkids' behavior? What if it's so damaging and out of control that their future as well as the future of your marriage are at stake? Stepmoms regularly deal with this development.

Sometimes Dad is struggling to parent his kids under a weight of guilt or lack of time, and he behaves more like a buddy than a parent, failing to set limits and make the hard decisions parents have to make. He may not listen to you anymore, but perhaps he'll hear someone outside the family. A friend or colleague could offer some commonsense guidance and help him see that his kids benefit from responsible parenting, and it's his job to provide it.

Some families have deteriorated so much that professional counsel is needed to help parents recognize destructive behaviors before the marriage is at risk. And if you're dealing with a husband who won't parent his kids or who blatantly uses different standards for what *his* kids are allowed to do or expected to do and what *your* kids are, then you know something has to change.

Nobody has to agree all the time and no utopia is coming to your home, but *both* parents in the home have to be willing to cooperate, compromise, and continue to make wise choices for the family to survive. A parent who fails as a parent will soon fail as a spouse, because a stepparent who's struggling not only against kids who have no limits, but against the immature and cowardly behavior of the parent, too, will look for relief soon.

I know that sounds harsh, but the you-against-them feeling is real and damaging to stepparents with the strongest of wills. And living like two families in one house won't work long. A stepfamily house divided will fall quicker than any other kind. And the cornerstone of support must be the marriage.

STEPPING STRONG. . .WHEN YOU STEP TOGETHER

Steplife spouses' support of each other is crucial and complicated. Parents may not know how to balance their loyalty to the kids and their loyalty to their marriage, but there's an easy test for most situations: What's good for your marriage is good for your kids. These behaviors from you and Dad will benefit everyone (and are predicated on loving stepparents devoted to their stepkids):

1. Respect each other's role. Kids need to see that the parents in the home are equally invested in the family and each other, that they form a dedicated leadership team, strong and solid. Let there be no question about your commitment to the future so that everyone feels secure. Support your spouse's authority and teach your children to respect it as well.

2. Support each other's decisions. When a stepparent makes a decision about a stepchild, she needs to do it with confidence and security. Parents who try to referee every stepparent/stepchild exchange and micromanage their relationship risk failure. Spouses need to trust one another so that the kids can trust whoever's not there to back up whoever is.

3. Confront each other privately. It's that unified front that's so important. Hash out your differences alone and then live the results out loud for the kids. If any gap shows—if anything prompts a hiccup—the kids may fear another divorce, or if that's what they want, they may try to exploit it. Let your words and actions speak only unity, stability, and agreement.

We consider blessed those who have persevered.
JAMES 5:11

Michele, a stepmom in England, practices looking past the pain, and she and her husband are making it work.

"We celebrate our second wedding anniversary next week, and it has been the hardest, most challenging two years of our lives. What has kept my husband and me staying in this relationship and persevering with the 'blending' (through kids having fights, the exes, our feelings about each other's kids, etc.) has been the incredible love my husband and I have for each other and our desire to be with each other.

"As my husband always says, 'When all this blending is over and the kids are fully grown, I want to be there to watch you grow old, both of us together.' This is what I look forward to and long for, and what keeps me together when at times I want to run to the opposite direction."

Modeling a good marriage is more beneficial to the kids than so much else we can do. When kids see parents who trust and honor each other, parents who take their responsibilities to each other seriously, parents who stick together no matter whose kid is in trouble, they see something they can believe in, something solid and permanent they can count on. They see hope for their own future.

CAN YOU CHECK THE "LIKES TO SHARE" BOX?

I used to wonder what I did with my time before my son was born. Then as a stepmom, I used to wonder why I thought scheduling was such a big deal before I had to manage it with a husband, an ex-husband, an ex-wife, and two more boys in the mix. Oh, the good ol' days. . .

Maybe getting your family all in one place on a holiday is a challenge you know well. Or maybe having to attend functions with people who don't like you (and whom you may not be too crazy about) is what keeps you up at night. Perhaps your aggravation is having no schedule at all, being at the mercy of everybody else, never able to make any plans, always the last to know and the first expected to bend. Oh, the days we have now!

"Bring them here to Me," He says. . . .

But rejoice! Things change. Even if it's tough now and you're juggling kids' schedules and dealing with broken plans, know that you'll get better at managing it and life will take care of some of the trouble. I know that may be little consolation right now, but fighting it only hurts you.

Sure, it may not be as fun to celebrate Christmas a week early or late, but it's the time together that counts, not the time of year. And birthdays still count even if the party has to be the day before or after. If you and Dad can alternate special days with Mom, that's great, but if the kids feel caught in a tug-of-war or have to interrupt their Easter morning to accommodate the grown-ups' argument, everybody suffers. Whenever you and your family celebrate events, focus on the content, not the calendar.

One of the little hidden joys of stepmotherhood is the expectation of your presence at your stepchildren's activities. We all know it. I've been to several football games, a Mother's Day church service, a few parties, two funerals, two graduations, and one wedding as the stepmom, with Mom there, too. We took care of our families together when her dad was terminally ill and when my husband broke his legs, and now we share our first grandchild.

Stepmom Michele had little time to prepare for her unavoidable encounter with her stepdaughters' mom. It wasn't pleasant.

"It is difficult to put into words the events of the past two years and how they have changed my life immeasurably. I met a wonderful man with two girls (aged twelve and ten), and I am also the mother of two girls. The challenge was that his two girls were the same age as mine, and they live full-time with him and so do mine.

"After dating for a few months, we got engaged and planned the beautiful wedding with our four gorgeous daughters by our side. Life was perfect, and I had visions and fantasies of my role as their 'mother' and my husband as my kids' 'father,' even though both exes had regular contact with our children!

"The fantasy was short-lived. It took about a week actually

for my world to come to a huge bump.

"The incredible challenge and responsibility of 'blending' the two families was *huge*. I think that it hit me about two weeks after we got married. I took some time off work to go to see my stepdaughter in a school assembly concert. I was ready to take my rightful place as her mum, right? I mean, I was bringing her up both physically and financially.

"Yet my stepdaughter came breezily up to me and said, 'Hi, Michele, come and sit next to my real mum,' and there was her biological mum sitting in prime position at her concert. It was a 'reality' slap in the face, and I learned that this was actually no romantic movie with lovey-dovey children and relationships. This was real, and actually in reality I was not their biological mother. I felt a fool."

You've been there, too. You've either taken your place alongside Mom, sat as far away from her as you could, or been the "mom" at your stepkids' events because she's not in their lives. All of it's tough. All of it demands your grace and patience, your willingness to hold your tongue and offer your hand. All of it gives you the opportunity to present a great example for the kids: one of poise under pressure, calm and control over your own behavior. You show them it's important to be there for the people in your life, even if it's a little uncomfortable. You play your role well and they see.

"Bring them here to Me," He says. . . .

And when we do, He supplies us with the guidance we need to keep our integrity, manage our expectations, and control our own behavior regardless of others' choices.

King Saul had pursued David, ready to kill him if given the opportunity. David, though, found the opportunity first. He didn't take it. He made another choice and left the rest to God.

> *"May the LORD judge between you and me. . .*
> *but my hand will not touch you."*
> 1 SAMUEL 24:12

That's our best choice, too, no matter how many Sauls we have in our lives. Our best choice is one of surrender to the work-in-progress concept our God has for us. He's made us, and He's made us to grow.

We learn that people will do what they please, and that may not be to our liking. We learn that circumstances aren't always what we'd choose. We learn that we have very little influence over some matters and that's just the way it is. We also learn something that will serve us well no matter what, that "the wise woman builds her house, but with her own hands the foolish one tears hers down" (Proverbs 14:1).

We can build or we can destroy. We can tend to "our house"—our integrity and our behavior—or we can argue about others' choices and fight what we can't change. We can gather all the broken pieces and uneven shards of everything that makes us want to scream and throw things, and we can give them to God. And in return, we know that the Lord is God—that He has made us and all the people in our lives, and He'll be by our side no matter what.

Is any one of you in trouble? He should pray.
Is anyone happy? Let him sing songs of praise.
JAMES 5:13

When we "bring them here to Me," we lay it all down, turning to God with the trust He craves, the heart that's fearful, and the family we want to grow. We know we can't do it alone, and we finally believe we don't have to. So we give our best efforts, learning every day and getting better as we go.

Still, the hurt comes now and then. A new situation lands hard, the tenuous grasp we have on our world slips, and we start to fall. We know very little, but we know enough, that God's in control, shepherding a flock forever in need of His unending grace, guidance, and goodness. We don't have all the answers, but He does, and that means we'll be okay. We can make it now, turning to Him, alone no more.

I have made you and I will carry you;
I will sustain you and I will rescue you.
ISAIAH 46:4

Chapter 5

We are His people and the sheep of His pasture.
Psalm 100:3 NKJV

⟨ . . .OH, SO I DON'T HAVE TO BE IN CONTROL?

"Bring them here to Me," He said. . . .

I won first place in a quilt show once. Oh, it was a beauty, one I'd made for my husband. I had dreamed about winning from the day of his birthday in February until my town's Heritage Day Quilt Show in November. I had a really good feeling about this one. Since I'd won third place the previous year and I thought this was a much better quilt, I harnessed my optimism like a five-year-old with a runaway locomotive.

I watched the parade, bought my yearly supply of vanilla flavoring from the ladies with the bonnets, and headed south on the sidewalk. I knew the ribbons would be lovingly placed on the quilts, spaced out on metal tables in the City Hall across from the fire department's antique tractor exhibit. I wandered in so cool, you should have seen me. Then I saw my quilt. And I saw the ribbon on top of it. It was blue.

Are you happy for me? I was, until I realized that my quilt was the only one in its category. There's nothing like a lack of competition to take all the fun out of winning.

I remember the day I surrendered control of my steplife to God. Oh, I know I never really had the ultimate control I wanted. But I certainly tried hard enough to get it, to the point of blaming God when I couldn't and making everybody around me miserable while I tried even harder. I fought and fought to "fix" everything by putting my hand on it all, shaking it hard if it didn't work right, and shooing away anything that dared to interfere. Well, you can just imagine how successful I was.

It's perhaps the stepmom curse. But we mean well, really. We want to help. Sometimes we want to be the savior everyone's looking for when wounds are deep and hearts are hurt. We might even think it doesn't look that complicated, on the outside looking in, mentally noting the rip we'll repair here, the tear we'll stitch up there. But somehow things don't work out just like we see in our heads. Pretty soon, steplife is like hanging from our split ends on an out-of-control roller coaster. The upset stomach is nauseating in its loyalty, and that pain in the neck feels like those sharp bones when the pork chops are cut wrong. Still, we struggle, we cry, we hurt, and we wonder. And finally, we get enough.

We get enough of the despair, the worry, the fear, and decide it has to stop. We know we can't go on living that way. I knew it. I knew that day I couldn't fight it anymore, that day I had to stop demanding something of God and start listening to Him. I knew that day that if I didn't partner with God in this steplife, I'd be living some other kind of life alone. I knew I didn't want to fail. And God told me how to succeed. I was looking in the wrong place. It wasn't about the other quilts. It was only about *mine*.

I couldn't succeed by making everything work out to suit me. I couldn't succeed by forcing the people in my life to conform to my ideals. I couldn't succeed if I dressed us all up to show the world how well we'd all melted into one. It was much bigger and much smaller than all that at the same time.

The success I wanted wasn't something I could touch. It was something I had to feel inside, guided by God as I trusted *Him*, just Him and me. It was that small.

And it wasn't something I could contain. It was something I had to live, reflecting God to those around me, to everyone in my messy life. It was that big.

He made my part specific and manageable for this confused and dizzy disciple. He said turn to Him and surrender to Him. Let Him worry about everything I can't understand, let Him carry this burden and do His job, let Him be in control and love me through it all. *"Bring them here to Me. . ."* I said okay.

We fight that surrender sometimes because it sounds like we're giving up, admitting this life will never be any better than the last battle with a stepchild or the still raw heartbreak caused by her dad. Why bother?

But our surrender to God is not defeating; it's defusing. The bomb's no longer a threat.

The constant fear of many stepmoms is that they're one word, mistake, or meltdown away from their world exploding. Maybe to everyone on the outside, a stepmom can live on the edge, quite convincingly even—a play with scenes rehearsed enough to fool every critic. But behind closed doors, she knows every thought and action is a short-circuited wire ready to take it all down.

That kind of performance is hard to pull off and harder to live up to. I know. And I know the only way to keep going is to dismantle the fear, defuse the bomb I've built myself that threatens to blow up in my heart and home. That defusing comes not with more fighting, grasping, and struggling, but only with surrendering. This means surrendering not to the situation, or your stepkids, or their mom, and not to the wounds still bleeding from the latest wreck—but to God and God alone. Then the pressure's off. You can breathe.

"The LORD reigns, let the nations tremble" (Psalm 99:1), the psalmist says. And so do we. With surrender to His control, we gain His protection. He is both shield for us and shatterer of the explosives in our heart. "Take that, you bomb!" we can say. He reigns in your family, too, and all that would threaten it trembles at His breath.

Stepmom Tami lives this practice.

"Unless you surrender to God any anger or bitterness or unforgiveness (all of which I have felt in varying forms once I became a stepmom), you will end up miserable and hopeless (which I have been also). I find that when I surrender to God's authority, He will be my healer, my redeemer, my rock, and my fortress. He alone has the authority to judge or punish, so I give it to Him and He takes care of all of it."

Our surrender changes our lives. We partner with God instead of trying to persuade Him to do our will. We seek His presence and find comfort and sustenance there, regardless of the circumstance. We give all the mess, worry, and damage to Him and trust He will give us His guidance and grace in return.

The deal may not look very fair, but He doesn't seem to mind. Apparently our turning to Him in trust and need is sweet manna to Him—a miracle of its own that unleashes more in every wrinkle of our lives. This surrender frees us to fully take hold of our steplives, to embrace and expand them with newfound courage, energy, and peace.

Struggles remain, of course. People love us or they don't. Some things about this life we'll never understand or master. But within the tiny sphere that we can make stable, in the places we can touch, God accepts our willingness and gives us work.

It may or may not look a lot like what we've been praying so hard for, but it's never unsupervised. It might even be surprising now and then, because our surrender gives us permission to do so many things, things we might not have allowed ourselves to do earlier. When we've been deep in fear, resentment, pain, or anger, the very choices that could have helped us the most, feel like the hardest ones to make. Our choice of surrender changes all that, and we are freed by God's love and grace to turn where we are into where we want to be. No, not in charge, but in concert with the One who is, we have permission to *forgive*, permission to *wait*, and permission to *give*.

⊙ PERMISSION TO FORGIVE

Rebecca Hopersberger, stepmom to two boys, knows sustaining peace found in only this hard-to-reach place.

"The hardest part of my journey toward a peaceful life as a stepmother has been tackling forgiveness. Regardless of the amicability of the situation, there are always hurt feelings that run deep. The best of situations can leave us dragging around a bag of hurt and anger that also happens to be a constant reminder that we were not the first wife or the children's 'real' mother.

"When I finally started to understand true forgiveness, I found myself in a position where I was better able to work/deal with my stepsons' mother.

"Despite our best intentions, none of us is ever fully prepared to be the second wife, let alone the stepmother. With love in our hearts and stars in our eyes, we marry the man of our dreams and think that all of our love will solve all of our problems. Once the buzz wears off, we are left with an amazing hangover and a whole host of emotions that not only are we unprepared for but that we have no clue what to do about.

"I have believed for some time that all of the misery my stepsons' mother wrought upon our family was completely one-sided. To a great extent, it was, in that we did not allow our actions to be as affected by our emotions as she did. However, none of us exists in a vacuum, and the sheer presence of hostile emotion (regardless of a person's actions) poisons relationships. I have never been good at being fake, and it wouldn't have taken a psychic to figure out that I had a lot of anger toward my stepsons' mother. There are some days I still do. My emotions are so raw and real that they are almost tangible, and I know she sensed it.

"I had tried to reach out to her before. I had tried to make things better for everyone, but at one point about a year ago, things changed. I was driving in my car, and like most days when I actually get some time to myself, I was pondering our situation—not just pondering, I was praying. Suddenly, I was overcome with emotion. As tears rolled down my cheeks, I felt a kind of understanding that I hadn't felt before.

"Being a Christian woman, I knew why I was flooded with emotion: God was answering my prayers, and I had finally found the time to listen. So much of my alone time for so many years has been spent in prayer, and an overwhelming majority of those prayers have been for my stepsons and their mother. As I cried, my heart listened, and I understood that God needed me to forgive her.

"I have often lamented the fact that my husband lost a great deal of his innocence to his first wife. More than that, I have spent a lot of years angry, angry with her for doing what she did. I was angry because she never seemed sorry for what she did to my husband or her children (at least never appeared sorry).

"Deep down I have always known that the path to a better relationship with my stepsons' mother would be found through forgiveness. Oh boy, is that hard. That day, as I listened to God's voice, I believe I truly understood for the first time what forgiveness is really about.

"I realized that God wants us to forgive others so that we may lighten our own burden. God loves us, and He knows the weight of so much anger is a terrible load to carry each day. Forgiveness is not for those who need to be forgiven; it is for those of us who need to forgive.

"My prayers were answered that day when I began to understand that the only way for things to truly get better is for me to let go of some of the anger and hurt that I have—and forgive my stepsons' mother.

"So I have.

"She doesn't know it. She probably doesn't think there is anything that she needs to be forgiven for, but I am confident that the air has changed. There is far less anger and suspicion all around.

"The best part of where I am right now is that I am able to have conversations with her that don't make me want to pull my hair out. Giving her the benefit of the doubt allows me to spend less time worrying and speculating as to what future conflict there may be.

"The most important part of this is that I understand that I can be nice, work with her, and even trust her a little bit, all without putting my guard down. There are a lot of things that end up being just plain petty when you think about it. I am now able to look at things, determine their worth in the grand scheme, and simply let the little stuff slide because there isn't some sort of running tally sheet fueled by stored-up anger. Forgiving her doesn't mean that I forget what she is capable of or what she has done in the past. It simply gives me the ability to be more human and not carry around so much emotional baggage all the time.

"This has been a little harder for my husband. While he totally, 100 percent agrees with me and supports my new approach, he has a much harder time with the forgiveness part of it. I really don't blame him. I will never know what it was like for him to live through his divorce. He has a lot more to forgive, and I completely expect his journey to be a longer one. Still, I have faith in him. He is an amazing man, and I know that God's love for him will send him on the right path."

◯ STEPPING STRONG. . .WHEN FORGIVING IS HARD

God has given us the capacity to forgive the deepest wounds, but it's up to us to activate that forgiveness. Here are a few tips that might help.

1. Forget forgetting. Painful memories don't just die, as much as we wish they did, and pressuring ourselves to behave as if they have is more pressure than we need. Acknowledge what's happened, but don't live by reliving bad experiences. They *are* in the past, and learning to leave them there doesn't mean pretending they don't exist. You just allow yourself to move on.

2. Realize your limitations. We don't know everything about everything, but God does. That makes Him much abler to handle our hurts, so we can give them to Him with confidence and relieve ourselves of the need to make sense of things that just don't make sense to us.

3. Keep beginning again. Today may not be a day you can forgive well. A memory that

won't be quiet, a new hurt that pushes you
down, an effort shoved back at you broken—
everything hard makes forgiving harder, but
every day is a new start. Accept your progress
today, and start fresh tomorrow.

Bear with each other and forgive whatever grievances you may
have against one another. Forgive as the Lord forgave you.
COLOSSIANS 3:13

PERMISSION TO WAIT

Canadian stepmom Mary has waited through much, and
waits now for more.

"Well, after many years, things have turned around and
everyone gets along!

"My husband and I had a stillborn baby boy in 1995. That
was so traumatic for the whole family. Even so, the situation
with my husband's ex-wife and my oldest stepdaughter,
Linda, did not really improve. After losing our baby,
everything seemed worse.

"In November of 1996, we had another baby boy,
Kevin, and everything went well! The three 'sisters' are all
pretty crazy about him, but I was still having problems with
the oldest daughter. She is fifteen years older than Kevin.

"About three or four years ago, it suddenly seemed as if

the oldest girl was finally starting to come around, and we noticed a big improvement in her attitude. Still, the ex-wife was trying to cause problems on a regular basis. . . .

"I was diagnosed with breast cancer in 2005 and was given six days to decide whether I wanted a mastectomy with chemotherapy or a lumpectomy with chemo and radiation. I ended up going with the latter. I was operated on exactly ten years to the day that I had come home after losing our first dear little boy. That was very, very difficult. I couldn't stop thinking about that. My family and friends really helped me through a rough time, and yes, even Linda, my oldest stepdaughter! I never really had a problem with the two younger daughters.

"Well, Linda became engaged in 2007 to a very nice fellow and set a date for the wedding. Somehow she must have had a big talk with her mom about all the bad things that had happened. In the end, her mom made her a gorgeous wedding dress to sort of 'make up' for everything that had gone wrong.

"We all went to the wedding. It was a five-hour drive or so, and it was in December, not long before Christmas. Needless to say, here in Canada, the weather was a bit of a factor, and we hit a big storm on the way back. But the main thing is that at the wedding and reception, everyone talked together. Linda's mom and I actually got along quite well, and the groom's parents were there, so we had fun with them. Everything was great!

"Since that event, things have really changed. I can tell that the tension is gone. Sometimes I have even spoken to my stepdaughters while they're at their mom's house, and there are no longer any 'big secrets.' It is so much more enjoyable now to spend time with them or have them visit!

"This past weekend, I drove down to where Linda is living (about six hours by car) to go to her baby shower. One sister couldn't go, but the middle stepdaughter was there (in fact, she invited me to stay overnight on the way down). We had a great evening and I took loads of photos, yes, even of Linda's mom! This baby will have three sets of grandparents!"

STEPPING STRONG. . .WHEN SETBACKS KEEP COMING

Getting to a peaceful place in your stepfamily may be like getting to the sandbar way out from the shore. There is a strong undertow, and sticky jellyfish lurk beneath your steps. Where we want to be is always there, and we can keep going no matter what keeps coming.

1. Assess the landscape. Setbacks come for "regular" families, too. Take stock of what's happening outside of your control that could be affecting everything: people change, job pressures mount, and kids become teenagers. Realize how much of your life may be more *regular* than *step*.

2. Assess your influence. How much have you contributed to any setbacks, and how will you work to counter the next one? No, you can't change circumstances, but you can offer a new perspective, clear up misunderstandings, learn from your mistakes, and encourage others to deal with the crisis and move on to better times. *You* can be a stable port in your family's storms.

3. Assess the canvas. Maybe recurring issues in your family lead to frequent setbacks. Are you and Dad constantly sending mixed signals to the kids? Is the acquiescence to Mom's demands creating deep resentment in your household? If you seem to fight the same fight over and over again, clean up the battlefield and end that war.

Set an example for the believers in speech,
in life, in love, in faith and in purity.
1 TIMOTHY 4:12

◯ PERMISSION TO GIVE

Stepmom Kathy, with six kids, knows about giving, without asking anything in return.

"Amazingly, from the very beginning of bringing all six kids together, they got along. Not to say there aren't 'issues,' but they really are the same issues you have with natural siblings. My relationship with my stepkids can be summed up in the fact that it waxes and wanes, which I have come to trust and believe is normal, natural, and expected. I am not the easiest person to get along with. I have expectations and have no problem taking charge.

"Well, that happens to be exactly what my stepkids were *not* used to. I had the challenge of running the household, not compromising the way I parent my own children, and building a relationship with my stepchildren. Just to put a visual to that, it's like walking a tightrope that periodically shoots electrical impulses and the balance bar is weighted on one side, so you are constantly trying to counterbalance your balance bar, and the out-of-balance side is your own children.

"What I was able to do is to realize that the kids have two parents. Although the mother is not a part of their daily life, she and my husband are the ones responsible for their outcome. At the same time, I didn't want to take away from the kids that which I saw and knew needed to be corrected or tweaked.

"We have experienced different levels of problems and

minor crises (at kid level), and I have stepped in as I would for my own children. However, there have been times when I just wanted to turn my back because it's way harder to parent someone else's children. You don't do it with the same passion.

"All I could think of was how bad I would feel later in life if they did not have these skills because their parents didn't have them to teach, and I had the opportunity to give them. As we conquer these situations, I always take the time to explain to the kids about the punishment, or why we had to talk about it, or the bigger picture and how I as an adult and a parent can see it so differently. I know this has built trust within my stepkids, to the point that my sixteen-year-old stepson confided only in me for eight months about a crush he was having at school.

"My other stepson loves that I am involved in his daily life and know all of his friends and the parents, and he is thrilled when I suggest he invites some kids over to hang out. I really felt that closeness one day when he was at a friend's sleepover. It was his mother's weekend, and she wanted to pick him up from the sleepover but didn't know where the house was, so she followed me because we are close friends with the family. When we got there, the kids were playing outside, and everyone looked at my stepson's mother with the look of 'Who is that?' and he said, 'For any of you who don't know, this is my mom.' The kids took a minute to register that, because they see me as his mom although they 'know' I am his stepmom, but I am the one there at school and games and events.

"Lastly, my stepdaughter is ten, and just the other day her mom came up for a visit. They had her ride on the float I and the kids were on, which was fine. She lives ninety miles from where we live, so she didn't know anyone. I thought it must have seemed very odd to her. Anyway, my stepdaughter literally did not talk to me and acted as if I didn't exist.

"I know it is difficult for kids in those situations, so I let it be. Then I talked to my sister, who pointed out, 'Look how much she trusts you—she knew that if she didn't talk to you, you would still love her at home, and with her mom, she won't rock the boat at all for fear that her mom will get mad.' I realized I have given the kids confidence and security, and I know this is God's plan for me with them."

STEPPING STRONG. . .WHEN GIVING DOESN'T GIVE BACK

Sometimes giving isn't easy, but it's never wrong. And we can learn how to do it better.

1. Give in concert with God. When we give of ourselves as part of our partnership with God, we give without worrying about who's looking, because we're looking at *Him*. Our giving isn't an act of our own, but a distribution of God's good wishes. And that makes giving an honor.

2. Give to make room for more. We gain nothing by hoarding our riches, tangible or otherwise. We will only receive more grace, compassion, understanding, joy, and peace when we give away what we've already been given.

3. Give to form the habit. Our giving is about us, not the people we give to. If we stop to weigh the possible benefits of our giving, we may miss the opportunity. But if we choose each morning to give throughout the day, we'll come to act and react out of habit, giving where we can without focusing on someone's response. That part can be God's job.

*By his power he may fulfill every good purpose of
yours and every act prompted by your faith.*
2 THESSALONIANS 1:11

☾ SURRENDERING TO JOY

Most people wouldn't need to have a blueprint for joy,
but hey, I can complicate a throw pillow. Imagine a fragile
stepfamily in my hands. I had a plan for everyone's instant
joy, happiness, peace, and all around giddiness that I figured
should take about a month, maybe less. Task-oriented
commandant (though loved and cherished by all, I was sure)
that I was, I set out to achieve this state of unbelievable bliss
and decided not to bother God with a lot of pesky details. I
had it covered.

But it was covered with anything but joy. No need to get
specific. That short month I thought we'd need was just a
brutal kick to sudden death overtime. There were flags all over
the play.

*When I said, "My foot is slipping," your love, O LORD,
supported me. When anxiety was great within me,
your consolation brought joy to my soul.*
PSALM 94:18–19

There is great joy in falling into God's protective arms,

great peace in leaning into Him and trusting Him to be there. Being in control of my own neurotic self is enough of a chore. I don't need to take on the rest of my family. When I realized that, I think I breathed for the first time in four or five years. We discover great joy in releasing a burden, even one we've created, tended, fed, and watered ourselves.

We can be who God already sees and wants to use no matter how full of anxiety we are or how badly we've messed things up so far. We worship the God of first, second, and hundredth chances, always ready to console us, never withholding the joy that's ours when we see that it's Him— Him close to us, strengthening us, showing us how to deal with today and tomorrow.

And so very often, that dealing comes by taking a few steps back. I think perhaps the psalmist's foot was slipping because he was treading where he shouldn't have been, teetering on the edge of a really big disaster because he was going too far. Whew, I've been there. I've fallen off that jagged cliff a few too many times because I never bothered to look for help. I didn't have time for joy. Are you kidding? It's tough to rest in God's peace and presence when you're stretching over that canyon like some kind of rubber toy, about to stretch in two and lose parts of yourself, but you're too stubborn to pull back.

Oh yeah, I'm your perfect example. Any happiness I felt had to come at the appointed time, after I'd arranged everything, solved everybody's problems, anticipated any new problems, and carefully orchestrated everyone's actions so that nobody could bother anybody else. Heaven forbid they actually learn to accept one another or work out their differences without my valuable interference, which was less subtle than a bulldozer.

That's exhausting. And it's not very joyful. But what could I do?

I wanted to be the stepmom who avoided all the stereotypes and stumbles of my predecessors. I wanted to leave all my mistakes and misgivings behind and see only a new record of all right-doing. I wanted to be joyful, sure, but that could only follow my flawlessness. And if I was the perfect stepmom, then my family would follow suit and my work would be done. Simple.

I explained that to God. It turned out He had a few things to explain to me. My joy wouldn't come in fixing everyone else or even myself, but in surrendering all of us to Him and constantly walking with Him to be what He chose.

Letting Him take on the world and all the imperfect stuff in my little part of it felt like taking off a pair of fifty-pound earrings. I could stand up straight and look ahead, trusting God to tend His sheep as He saw fit and living in the joy He promised.

Surrender wasn't failure but *focus.* Focus on Him instead of me, on accepting His work in the fertile ground of my heart so that others could see. Maybe when I get myself all tended to, I can move on to someone else. Of course, I'll have great-grandchildren by then, but stay tuned.

◯ STEP STOP

Realizing we can't do everything on our own is a little depressing, for a second. Then with the next breath comes the relief that we don't have to do everything, and God has designed it that way. Paul wrote about his and Timothy's hardships in their work and what that taught them—"that we might not rely on ourselves but on God" (2 Corinthians 1:9).

When we're fighting our own hardships, we can choose to rely on ourselves or on God. In every situation, in every second, we'll make that choice. We'll choose between horror and hope. We'll choose between greed and grace. We'll choose between our madness and His methods. We'll do it every day and live with that decision. Hardships are waiting for our prayers, or pressure from us.

Go ahead, choose.

Turning to God with our complete surrender doesn't banish from our lives all the difficult people and real problems we have to deal with, but it helps us banish a few other, perhaps far more damaging threats to our peace and joy.

He reached down from on high and took hold of me; he drew me out of deep waters. He rescued me from my powerful enemy, from my foes, who were too strong for me. They confronted me in the day of my disaster, but the LORD *was my support. He brought me out into a spacious place; he rescued me because he delighted in me.*
PSALM 18:16–19

Those "foes" we need rescuing from first are of our own making: fear, insecurity, anger, worry, distrust, and jealousy. Our surrender to our God ushers us into a spacious place where peace, joy, graciousness, and courage can grow. He's already there to take hold of us and lead us through.

He's there to keep our focus on the quilt we make, on the category that holds just us. We can proudly display our blue ribbons as testimony to our progress. They represent not defeat for anyone else, but God's deepening design on our heart. That's all we need to keep stitching.

Stepmom Donna has her needle all threaded and ready to go.

"We're there: wonderful kids, wonderful stepkids, wonderful husband, and not-so-great ex-wife of his. But what is different from then and now is that I am doing better handling what she sends our way, or better yet, what she *tries* to send our way. My husband, our kids, and I are going to a church that is perfect for all of us.

"And I know that just letting myself let go and letting God take over all aspects of our life is what we all needed."

Donna knows. It's not a victory over the people in our lives that we need so desperately, but a victory over the *power* we give to the people in our lives. When we surrender, we stop fighting. We focus on *God's* power and complete control. He's not scared, and we don't have to be either. And that's reason for many thanks.

Be joyful always; pray continually; give thanks in all circumstances, for this is God's will for you in Christ Jesus.
1 THESSALONIANS 5:16–18

Chapter 6

Enter into His gates with thanksgiving,
and into His courts with praise.
Be thankful to Him, and bless His name.
PSALM 100:4 NKJV

○ . . .BUT WHERE'S THE COMPLAINT DEPARTMENT?

How do your prayers begin? Are they constant, as you rest in God's presence and give thanks for all you see and all to come? Are you praying in peace because God seeks your prayers, or are you praying in confusion sometimes, confident of God's control but—because that human part of us still talks back with such snarkiness—unable to see how He'll make sense of all the mess and guide you to do the same?

Those prayers of fear and desperation may always be part of a stepmom's life, and through them we learn much and continue to grow in our compassion and understanding. But what we discover is that our prayers become lopsided, like a teamster and a toddler carrying a china cabinet. One side carries the weight and supports the other.

The gratitude of our prayers grows muscles as we put it to work, and it carries every other emotion we have. With our fears and desperation supported, surrounded, and sustained by our gratitude, God can do His job and lead us to do ours. Just like the moving duo, the job gets done and nothing gets broken.

Jesus told us all about the value and effectiveness of gratitude. He framed many of His most eloquent words around the bounty of blessings our Father gives us and shows us how to put those blessings into practice every day. When we replace our panic with praise, we live the peace of a life respondent to God, and gratitude overflows. Here's how.

Remember who you are—a beloved daughter of the King of kings, and nothing changes that. No steptrouble, no interfering extended family, no ungrateful kids—*nothing*—can take away our place in those gates and courts of His. Jesus spoke about those who only pray to be heard, with little thought to whether God would listen or care or act. No, no, He says.

"Do not be like them, for your Father knows what you need before you ask him" (Matthew 6:8). So that's how we know. We know God's already there, in charge, in control, wherever we are. He's guarding the gates and watching everything, surprised by nothing we can think, say, or need. That's because of *who you are*, the child He cannot forget, and *who He is*, the Keeper of all you need. Let's give thanks.

Rely on Him for all you need, for everything you see and, mercifully, everything you don't. We could spend all our time worrying if we wanted to. Lord knows there's enough stuff falling down around us every day to snap all our brain cells to attention and mount them up on a steed of stressful anxiety. The demands from those around us are heavy and constant. Let's remember that God's vision is bigger than ours, with a plan already in place to quell any uprising.

"Look at the birds of the air; they do not sow or reap or store away in barns, and yet your heavenly Father feeds them. Are you not much more valuable than they? Who of you by worrying can add a single hour to his life?" (Matthew

6:26–27). Don't you know God delights in us when we're as trusting creatures, too, when we take care of today with all He's given and trust Him for tomorrow? Don't you want that kind of rest and comfort, to know each day that your Father will surround you with the wisdom and abilities to live your stepmom role with grace and dignity? Know it and don't worry. Let's give thanks.

Relay Him to those around you, and watch when things begin to change. Sometimes we try so hard to make things better, to fix the problems around us, to be the backstop for all that would fall and break. Sometimes we make great progress with that, and sometimes we see our own limitations and wallow in regret and disappointment. But let's don't. Sure, we want to do all we can for our families. We want to solve problems and achieve goals. But it's not so much about checking items *off* a list. It's about reflecting our Father through everything *on* the list.

Jesus said, "In everything, do to others what you would have them do to you" (Matthew 7:12), and that keeps it pretty simple. When we look at everything that's broken, we see too many places to touch, too much damage to contain. But we can narrow our focus and look at everything that's within our power to touch, and then we can touch it with God.

We don't have to be politician or surgeon, police officer or savior, but we can relay to those around us His love and grace through our actions, simple and pure. We can take our cues from God—who will never fail to direct us—and we can reflect Him in all we do. That's all. He takes care of the rest. Let's give thanks.

⟳ STEPPING STRONG. . .WHEN RELAYING GOD TO OTHERS IS NOT WHAT THEY WANT

How can we go forward with this great privilege and responsibility when everything we do seems to trigger only contempt or scorn from kids and their parents alike? Well, we keep doing what we're doing and make sure there are a few things we don't do.

1. Don't preach. Our best sermons are unspoken.
2. Don't judge. It's a heavy weight we can do without.
3. Don't worry. God's will is stronger than anyone's "won't."

It's funny. As we practice our *don'ts*, we'll see that we're still *doing* what He asks.

> *"If you utter worthy, not worthless, words,*
> *you will be my spokesman."*
> JEREMIAH 15:19

⌒ PERFECTION: DONE!

All this talk of what we can do or be careful not to do sounds like I'm asking a lot of you, doesn't it? It sounds like a lot to remember, a lot to master, a lot to handle when you already have more asked of you than any one person should have to endure. But if we'll wrap all we have to do within this perspective of peace and gratitude, we'll find ourselves surprisingly able to handle everything that happens with greater ease.

You may even surprise yourself when after a while, the same old arguments don't attack your sense of security like they once did. When the phone call from Mom doesn't make you sick to your stomach anymore, when another outburst from your stepson is something you can look at without fear, you will find that the changes *around* you mean little compared to the changes *within* you. You'll be living Jesus' admonition to "be perfect, therefore, as your heavenly Father is perfect" (Matthew 5:48).

Uh-oh, lost you there, didn't I? Yes, you may agree that you've made great progress, but *perfect*? That's pushing it a bit, isn't it? Jesus came because we aren't perfect in the unblemished, flawless sense of the word, and we need Him to save us. And because He did, we can partner with Him to become perfect in the learning, striving, maturing, and reflecting sense of the word. That's what God's asking for, and that's what we can deliver.

Every day we can choose to become more like Him as we *remember* who we are, *rely* on Him for all we need, and *relay* Him to those around us. Every day we can choose to respond with thanksgiving and praise, do what He says, and leave everything else alone, living our role in the perfection He seeks. We can do that.

⟲ WHAT DO YOU WANT?

Just as our stepfamily blending takes time, so does our quest for perfection, and amazingly, God lets us pick the timetable for it all. He's not expecting you to be the World's Greatest Stepmom today, or ever. He's not standing over you with a list of actions to get you to some place of peace, though we all want that. He's not keeping score of every "perfect" or "impressive" thing you do—wish we could say the same. No, He's waiting for you to make the next move.

So how do we start? Do we want to be there, perfect with God? asks Jesus.

During his teaching time in Jerusalem, Jesus encountered people seeking healing at the pool called Bethesda, "the blind, the lame, the paralyzed" (John 5:3). One may have waited there for thirty-eight years. We've had some of those stepmom years that count like dog years, haven't we, some of those days so ugly they'd stop an eight-day clock, days that can make us feel like we've waited for healing for a *hundred* and thirty-eight years. . . Sorry, back to the story.

When Jesus came upon that man, He was apparently able to tell that the man had homesteaded that area for a while, and asked him bluntly: "Do you want to get well?" (John 5:6).

And so He asks us. Do we want to get well? Do we want to be perfect, or are we content beside the healing waters? Do we want to live in gratitude and joy? Do we want to risk the failure, make the effort, face our fears, and get better? Then we have to move, He says. The man told Jesus that he couldn't move.

He told the man, "Get up! Pick up your mat and walk" (John 5:8). Don't wait—move now, He says. Depending on others isn't working. Being in almost the right place won't do. Poor excuse or no excuse, it doesn't matter. *Move!*

And that's what we can do. That's where we can put our faith to work and become a stepmom with goals, with a plan. The healing pool is waiting.

We need that blessed water to save us from ourselves, from the mistakes we've come to know well and have the habit of repeating. Jesus' plan works for us when steplife is playing itself out with a vengeance, riding in like high tide spreading disrespect, rejection, distrust, anger, and selfishness. We can accept God's healing at that moment of interaction with the kids or their mom or anyone else, if that's what we want.

How about you? What will you do the next time the waters are stirred?

Don't wait. When the opportunity comes, use that time to

show your stepkids who you are, to demonstrate your choice to do the right thing, to respond with restraint and integrity, to trust in your God.

Don't depend on others. Let your family members see you're strong enough to step out on your convictions, secure enough to risk making a tough decision, and willing to work hard or sacrifice for them.

Don't doubt in a new situation. "At once" the man obeyed Jesus and results came. Rely on what you know to get you closer to where you want to be, even an unexpected turn in the road.

STEPPING STRONG. . .WHEN THE PLAN BACKFIRES

Maybe a particular episode brings not progress but pain: a fight with your stepdaughter, a run-in with Dad, an unexpected visit from Mom, or a weekend that makes elective surgery sound tempting. Don't panic; replan.

1. Do an autopsy of the situation, from an objective point of view, after you've calmed down. Give yourself time.

2. Don't obsess. Don't give more weight to a comment or event than it warrants. I'll guarantee that the other party isn't.

3. Get ready to *move*. Clear up or rectify any misconstructed words or deeds and then grab on to your hope. Express that hope to the other person if you can.

4. Get ready to *move on*. Trust God with this situation and all the rest. Maybe you can't depend on next weekend to be any different or on Mom to be more pleasant next time, but it doesn't matter. Trust God to meet you at the pool even if the worst happens. Do what you can, and He will do the rest.

When I called, you answered me;
you made me bold and stouthearted.
PSALM 138:3

GOAL #1: PERFECT SUCCESS

Maybe you'll feel like the invalid man: helpless, hopeless, unlikely to succeed, with no power and no leverage. That's okay, because our success will come from what we *give*, not what we take by force.

Our progress is measured by how much *we* change, not by how much our world changes. Our success, remember, is measured by God's scales, and His calculations work on an ironic method—the more we give away, the more we have.

So giving becomes goal number one, not because it's easy, and not because it's much fun or comfortable at first, but because it works. It releases us from one of the most damaging cancers of our role: selfishness. Certainly we need what we need to take care of ourselves and our family, and this isn't a discussion about child support or some admonition to you to let yourself be taken advantage of for the pleasure of others.

This discussion is about giving where you can and what you can because God has designed us that way—like faucets, not cisterns. And stepmoms aren't excused from this beauty of design. Give what you can, and your whole life—not just your steplife—will be better for it. God understands your life, so He knows where that will be difficult at first, but it's one of those self-fulfilling situations begun on trust and proven by results. Start small if you need to, but with big piles of belief, and you won't be disappointed.

One man gives freely, yet gains even more; another withholds unduly, but comes to poverty. A generous man will prosper; he who refreshes others will himself be refreshed.
PROVERBS 11:24–25

Your goal is perfection not in the flawless sense, but in the sense of progress in the present tense, every day a new plate of opportunity. Indulge all you want. Try everything. And more is guaranteed to come your way.

(STEP STOP

Sometimes we have to give from afar, because of either a physical distance or an emotional one. Our methods may change, but one constant remains: our prayers. We can withhold condemnation, speak only goodwill, and prepare for the reunion, physical or emotional, that we leave in God's hands. We can give from afar with no regrets.

We can pray this prayer for our family member:

May he give you the desire of your heart and make all your plans succeed.
PSALM 20:4

This prayer surrenders us and the person we're praying for to God, and His answer can only mean good things for us both. We trust He wants, plans, and will work toward only the best for us all, so when the *desires* of you and me and everyone else line up with God's, the outcome can only be more peace and more joy. Our gratitude overflows.

◠ GIVE, BUT YOU'RE NOT GOD

Our goals are to do what we can with God's help inside the bigger goal of leaving what we can't to God and trusting Him to show us the difference. Where we won't ever succeed is in trying to do anything without Him. But we can always remember to seek His guidance first and to thank Him for the help we trust is coming, for the solution He's working out, and for the plan that's always for our benefit.

Maybe your goal this week is to set some goals for yourself. May I make a suggestion? A great place to start is with a goal of finding the joy in *working toward* your goals. No, that's not spin or double-talk, just good planning.

Achieving our goals is great, of course, but things move slowly in stepmomland sometimes, and setbacks and interruptions to our plans are more likely than red tape at City Hall, and more trouble to work through. But God's commitment to us doesn't waver, and He asks us to see the good, the generous, the joyous, and the amazing along the way. He asks us to enjoy the view.

It may seem like your life is no longer your own when you become a stepmom: You have to check with everyone, plan around everyone, watch your mouth around everyone, and tiptoe around everyone or almost everyone. We all know how that is, but here's something we have to learn: Our lives actually become more our own than ever before, ours and God's, that is.

Maybe the metamorphosis is first for survival and then because you realize how productive and satisfying it is. You do your best with the kids and their mom and everyone else, and you're getting better at it every day, but you come to know that everything is somehow enveloped into the new and deepening enclave where you rest with God.

Whatever stepmom thing you have to do becomes less about the thing itself and more about what God's doing with it in the bigger picture that's your life. At first that seems scary, certainly unfamiliar—dangerous even. But we learn quickly, and God is present and presiding like the most devoted parent in the world. Oh, that's right—He is.

And so you're nestled in safety with permission to grow, overcome, explore, and *live* with a kind of abandon and trust you've never known. Nothing is just what it appears on the surface, and nothing is the horror you used to think it was. Everything is part of the whole, the whole that God's got His finger on and you know it.

That becomes your life that's more than it was before, because of the struggles and the victories, the life that no force outside you and God can threaten or damage, the life that brings you satisfaction and fulfillment as you and God work where He leads. Maybe nothing changes around you right now or right away, but it doesn't matter. It's not about change on the outside anymore; it's all about the inside. It works better that way. Goals abound, and you're ready.

STEPPING STRONG. . .WHEN NEW RESPONSES ARE REQUIRED

Our new way of life allows us to more easily develop new responses to old regrets, because we learn super quickly that striking out at others doesn't help a thing. Sometimes our biggest goal seems to be just to not make matters worse. Long-term solutions may require long-term thinking. It may take us awhile to be brilliant, but we can be these things now:

1. *Truthful.* Nothing is helped when we lie. We don't have to be cruel, but we need to be clear. Keeping up with lies and secrets takes energy we don't have.

2. *Objective.* Play the role of outsider at least for a moment, and take out as much emotion as you can when you're looking for a workable solution for everyone.

3. *Compassionate.* Everybody hurts, and where we can help, we should. Reflect God's compassion now, if not His understanding and guidance, because while those may take longer to get, it's worth the pursuit.

4. *Consistent.* Start with who you are and stay there. If something bothers you today, don't pretend it doesn't tomorrow to avoid a confrontation. Don't make the kids wonder which stepmom will show up. Sure, we compromise, but we keep our standards through every situation.

He who digs a hole and scoops it out falls into the pit he has made.
The trouble he causes recoils on himself; his violence
comes down on his own head.
PSALM 7:15–16

So when you and your husband are dealing with a teenager who lies or steals, or you're competing with an eight-year-old for your husband's attention, or her mom has again failed to send the information you need and she promised for the fifteenth time—when everything on the outside is just a big mess, you don't have to be.

The personalities and choices of all these people may make your life more, uh, challenging, but your goals remain. And no, we don't have a magic wand or remote control to point toward those disturbing situations, but we aren't without recourse. Pay attention to what you *do* have and find your peace there, even in the cyclone whirling around you.

You have choices. You can choose your words. You can choose your actions. You can choose to be brave. You can choose to be patient when you want to scream.

You have time. Most things short of fire and blood don't require an immediate response or resolution. Take the time to pray, study, plan, and recover so that you're better able to lead.

You have strength. Remember you don't face the mess alone. Your strength comes instantly with your breath of need. The strength of God is your strength to do the hard thing, to let go, or to hold on, whatever you need.

Practice finding gratitude in the hard days, not the easy ones. I know that sounds backwards, but in reality, it's a blessing. When we can face our most dreaded days with peace and the expectancy of God's hand on us, we'll find ourselves in such a habit of giving thanks that when our minds are idle in a respite, the reflex thought begins, "Thank You, Lord. . ." And we're chin-deep in joy in every circumstance.

◗ GOD'S IDEA

God is just full of ideas for helping us stepmoms stepmother more effectively. I'm sure He could use up all of the world's bandwidth if He sent us an e-mail with the list. How about we just pick a place to start, like our daily, hourly, moment-by-moment interaction with Him? Let's call it *praying*, *praising*, and *partnering*, and let's start now.

Stepmothering puts you squarely in God's kitchen like few other things. You're there: in the heat, too much work to do, not enough help, and wondering what to do next, every day. And while the idea of entering anything other than a solitary vacation with thanksgiving sounds impossible, if we'll *partner* with God as we *pray* nonstop, we'll overflow with *praise* like too much rice in a tiny pot. Only we won't make a mess.

With a little practice, we'll begin to see and live our lives—our *whole* lives, not just the stepmom part—in a new frame of gratitude and with a new intimacy with the God who is close enough to touch, the God who will listen to our complaints, silence our fears, guide our feeble steps, and laugh with us when we fall all over the blessings He spills along the way.

The constant awareness of God's presence and the new confidence with which we experience it bring to us unexpected power and joy, even in the midst of family problems that haven't gone away and family members who haven't changed. If we accept what He's offering and truly rely on Him for our direction, we see that He points us to Him, and that's where the help is. What a system.

Let the peace of Christ rule in your hearts. . .and be
thankful. . . . And whatever you do, whether in word
or deed, do it all in the name of the Lord Jesus,
giving thanks to God the Father through him.
COLOSSIANS 3:15, 17

I hear the "Yes, *but*. . ." coming from you already: "Yes, *but* there's too much to do for too many people, too much that's wrong, too much that's still not working to be very thankful or joyful."

I know. That's why God gives us every day, every opportunity, the entire rest of our lives to work it out, to understand, to fully grasp what it means to "enter into His gates with thanksgiving."

Being thankful for your disobedient stepdaughter is hard. Being thankful for what you have to handle it with isn't. God's hand will be on you while you deal with the situation. His guidance and instruction, the opportunity to use the experience to grow closer to her and to God, the chance to turn an unpleasant moment into a memory, the chance to laugh through a tough time or cry together until the two of you reach an understanding, the new practice you've mastered to respond with restraint, the words God has taught you that speak love and wisdom, your new maturity that allows you to assess the situation without falling apart—all of that is wrapped up in one experience, and as a stepmom you know you'll have a thousand more like it every day.

And when we approach those experiences from a place

of peace and gratitude, we get even closer to the God who is afraid of nothing, especially our problems that are way too big for us to carry alone. He sees us cry and sends help with a message: Cry no more.

After the Israelites under Nehemiah's command rebuilt the walls of Jerusalem, they gathered together to worship God. They felt the burden of the failures of their past, but God was focused on their future.

"Go and enjoy choice food and sweet drinks, and send some to those who have nothing prepared. This day is sacred to our Lord. Do not grieve, for the joy of the LORD is your strength."
NEHEMIAH 8:10

We'll gladly take the choice food and sweet drinks of steplife when they come our way. And we know how to appreciate every nourishing morsel—a little gratitude from a stepson, a word told in confidence by a stepdaughter, a show of trust from her mom, and we're full in the heart, ready to go forward another day. But what do we do with the other part of the charge, to "send some to those who have nothing prepared"?

Maybe that idea seems counterintuitive, to give what you've worked for away to someone who didn't make the effort. But what we learn is that what we pass on to others is what God has already given us. Then we are willing and eager, and our joy in all God's teachings and blessings has just *got* to come out in the way we live.

"Do not grieve, for the joy of the LORD is your strength."
NEHEMIAH 8:10

If we try to hold it in, we'll shrink from the inside out. But if we're strong enough to let it out, even through our wounds deep and raw, healing comes—healing for us and healing for others—because God sends our gifts where they need to go. We thank Him for the resources and opportunities He trusts us with, and we grow to see it's always enough.

So on an easy day or a hard day, "Thank You, Lord. . ." is the beginning and the end.

Let your gentleness be evident to all. The Lord is near. Do not be anxious about anything, but in everything, by prayer and petition, with thanksgiving, present your requests to God.
PHILIPPIANS 4:5–6

Chapter 7

For the LORD is good; His mercy is everlasting.
PSALM 100:5 NKJV

⌒ . . .SURE, HIS MERCY, BUT MINE IS RUNNING A BIT LOW

Sometimes the only thing that feels "everlasting" is the hurt that some parts of stepmothering inevitably bring. If your stepkids are small and you're struggling with custody arrangements and drained wallets, this time of stress and pressure may look "everlasting" to you, there on bended knee, energy and will slipping away faster than that one day of solitude you managed to carve out for yourself. And if that fear and uneasiness humming in the background like a fly caught between the windowpane and the screen seems "everlasting," know that a thousand other stepmoms are hearing the same noise and looking, just like you, for relief.

It's here.

God's everlasting help is here. He won't get scared by the problems in your family. He won't leave you to solve them alone. He won't decide you and your family aren't worth the trouble. Relax. Just keep doing what you're doing. Follow Him in everlasting trust and He'll show you what to do, guaranteed. But we must choose our way.

The story of the rich man who wanted to follow Jesus is often linked to our selfishness and greed, pointing out that we can't let anything we value of this world come between us and our Savior. In the story, Jesus tells the man that if he wants to follow Him, he'll need to give up everything else. "Then come, follow me," Jesus told him (Mark 10:21).

It was a lesson in trust, and the man didn't pass.

> *At this the man's face fell. He went away sad,*
> *because he had great wealth.*
> MARK 10:22

You might not look at what you have and hold right now as "great wealth," but the premise is the same. What are we willing to give up to do as Jesus says—to follow Him? What stepmom stuff will we part with, and what will we cling to? We have to choose before we can walk either path in front of us. We can take the road behind Jesus or the road alone with all our stuff. What do you have squirreled away in that bag?

Maybe you have some old hurts that still make you wince in pain. Maybe your stepdaughter's rejection is like a leech, draining blood from your heart every day. Maybe your stepkids' mom works overtime to turn the kids against you and they remain scared and suspicious of you. Maybe you give the kids all you are and all you have and they give you nothing in return—no appreciation, no recognition, nothing.

Maybe you just can't let go of the anger that lives in your heart like an intruder taking over your home at gunpoint. Maybe the kids refuse to respect your home, your space, and your authority, and their dad is no help. Maybe the courts are unfair in their judgments and fail to see Mom for what she is and the kids continue to suffer. Maybe the kids manipulate Dad and refuse to take responsibility for themselves and you're forced to be the only adult in the situation.

Maybe you still have dreams of a different life, a life that doesn't include all these problems. Maybe you thought stepmothering would be easier or more part-time or less of a burden on your marriage. Maybe you expected happily ever after, but you're lost somewhere in an awful wonderland and nothing makes sense anymore.

Maybe you're sick of the heavy, oppressive sense of the unfairness of it all. Unappreciated and overlooked, you feel stuck, not knowing what to do but not willing to admit nothing can be done. Maybe you truly are a victim of too many bad things and too many mean people, but living like one won't help.

Our living must reflect the victories we're achieving within ourselves. Our peace and joy must trump the pain and fear that others may represent. The steps we take to follow Jesus through the unexpected and the unbelievable must be steps of trust, faith, and courage, steps even now we sometimes take with tentative shuffles.

◯ STEPPING STRONG. . .WHEN YOU HAVE TO STAND UP

Stepmothering makes us better people in many ways, and if you've ever had a problem with standing up for yourself, you'll get over it pretty quickly as a stepmom. Everybody's learning how to live in the new family, and the battle lines get drawn deeply. Your goal, of course, is to make those lines disappear, but along the way, you have to take care of yourself.

1. Stand up from the top down. Start with what matters to you most. Don't tolerate lies, disrespect, or anything else that you believe is a fundamental deal breaker just to keep the peace temporarily. Make your point when the offense happens, explain it well, and hold on to it.

2. Stand up with a gentle step. Don't assume you'll have to come out swinging. Whatever gets to you may not be that big of a mess to correct if you seek cooperation and understanding among the kids and adults instead of starting with a knockout punch to everyone around.

3. Stand up by example. One of the best ways to influence the behavior of those around

you is to model right behavior for them. Let
yourself be the first place you won't tolerate
the words or actions you find intolerable in
others.

*"I am the LORD your God, who teaches you what is
best for you, who directs you in the way you should go."*
ISAIAH 48:17

Yes, the hurts still hurt. The situations that make us mad
are still there. The dreams we once dreamed are hard to wake
up from. But everything we hold on to that isn't propelling us
forward is pulling us back—everything. Let. . .it. . .go.

I know that sounds harsh and unfeeling, but please
understand that I've been there. I've petted those pains,
nursed that anger, and mourned those dreams until I thought
I would surely dehydrate from the truckloads of tears I cried.
And if it's possible to grow an ulcer from thoughts boiling
inside you, then I'm sure I cultivated quite a collection.

Often too afraid to hear myself say how I felt out loud, I'd
just digest it all like hidden grit in your salad. I wanted to get
past it all, really I did, but. . . And that's where I'd get stuck.
"Let's go over this one more time," I'd say to my weeping self,
"and be sure we don't forget a single hateful word or horrible
mistake. I can't let myself forget what everybody's done to me
or excuse anyone (me included) for this double root canal on
a loop that my life has become. God, are You *here*?"

And He was probably thinking, "Uh, yeah, I'm right

here, but you probably can't see around or over all that stuff you don't need. Maybe you could clean up a bit in here and then we could move on? Can we leave behind the bitterness, suspicion, blame, anger, insecurity. . .shall I go on?"

No, I got it.

So that's where we make our choice. We can stay there in the clutter and chaos (I've warmed it up for you, and don't be surprised if you even begin to feel quite comfortable there), or we can part with it all and follow our Father to somewhere much better. It's not a single destination, because He understands the constant state of change our steplives are in, and we may have to choose to let go and follow over and over again. But that's okay; that's progress.

◗ STEP STOP

Perfect is our pursuit. When Jesus changed Paul's life, Paul changed his ways.

"At once he began to preach in the synagogues that Jesus is the Son of God" (Acts 9:20). But those who heard were put off by this about-face from a persecutor of Christians.

> *All those who heard him were astonished and asked,*
> *"Isn't he the man who raised havoc in Jerusalem*
> *among those who call on this name?"*
> ACTS 9:21

Yes, those around Paul were skeptical, but we can *all* change, and with God's blessing, change for the better. How fortunate that will be for those around us.

> *Yet Saul grew more and more powerful and baffled the Jews*
> *living in Damascus by proving that Jesus is the Christ.*
> ACTS 9:22

Let's all work toward our goals and grow more powerful as disciples in stepmom gear. May we look at everything in steplife as a chance to show our families Christ reflected in our words, deeds, and choices. That's pretty perfect. Let's grow what we see and trust God to grow others as He pleases.

We've talked already about how the skills we develop as stepmoms make us smarter and stronger in every other aspect of our lives. Stepmothering didn't have to work very hard to make me more aware of my own room for improvement and change, but that was just me—not quite a throwback to Cinderella's day, but needy beyond measure all the same. Think of your worst mistake and double it. That was me.

Stepmothering forced me to live ideals I'd only proclaimed before. Stepmothering pushed me to limits I never would have approached otherwise.

And all the while I cried to God to do something with *them*, the new people in my life threatening to wreck all I was building. He didn't exactly answer the way I wanted. He focused on *me* with the kind of attention the "challenging" student gets in class, and I resisted. I shouldn't have. I only postponed the blessings He'd already prepared for me. What began as a plea for help with my stepfamily became answered prayer that molded a new me.

Stepmothering expanded my heart, of course, with love for my stepsons, but also with a broader way of looking at everything. I know that doesn't seem to connect, but because I had to learn to work around and through difficult situations and consider my opinions and responses from all angles, I became intimately aware of the intricacies of all kinds of issues in my life and in my interactions with others. My narrow point of view had to be usurped by the lens of stepmothering, and while I fought it at first, finally, after *years*, because I didn't get any faster, I began to see the value of it. I had to change my approach to everything steplife to survive, and after lots of practice doing that, I came to appreciate the residual effects.

Particularly the conscious choice to pause before I panicked when something happened and to wait—just wait—before having a fit, rocketing to conclusions, or making plans served me so well in my steplife dramas that I tried it on for size in other arenas. And guess what? God was there in all of those situations, too. Shocker, I know.

He was there calming me and keeping me from reverting to the old me who would react with Olympic-medal speed and bring even more chaos to the situation. That one wonderful skill or habit or whatever you want to call it, prompted, guided, and sustained by God, is something I might never have developed were I not a stepmom. Now, of course, I like to think my supreme spirituality would have brought such maturity to pass regardless of my marital status, but I kinda doubt it.

I imagine you have your own exposed blessings, or maybe you're developing a new skill now that serves your stepmothering well and will find its way into the rest of your life. Think about that as we look at a few other ways God's everlasting fingerprint is on everything we do.

◯ TRUST

Gideon was an unlikely hero. He wasn't the first choice many of the Israelites would have made for defeating the neighboring Midianites. When God gave him that job, Gideon was confused. "But, Lord," Gideon asked, "how can I save Israel? My clan is the weakest in Manasseh, and I am the least in my family" (Judges 6:15).

Gideon had no college education, no superior strength, no connections with government officials, and yet God chose him to beat back the invading Midian army. He even reduced the force Gideon had from 32,000 to 300. God wanted to prove that His strength and ability alone saved His people, so He sent an undersized army in the hands of an underdog leader for an unexpected victory, all to accomplish His will. All Gideon had to march on was his trust and what God gave him. That was enough. It's enough for us, too.

When you're invaded by lies about you from your stepkids' mom or manipulation by a stepchild who wants you away from her dad, stop and look at your situation. Can you fix it all by yourself? Are you big enough or crafty enough to make people fall in line and do your bidding like the crooks in the movies who swindle and trick everyone? No, and that's not how God works. He gives us what we need to do our part in the battle while He manages and maneuvers the whole situation as He sees fit.

Yes, we have a job to do in these injustices, but our

biggest job is trusting God with them. We use what we have, what He gives us, and we don't try to manufacture more. Take stock of what you have, and prepare.

PREPARATION

The time for war was now for Gideon. He couldn't wait, he couldn't run, he couldn't avoid it. We know that feeling, don't we? We know when the weekend is coming and uncooperative stepkids will crash through our doors. We know when court dates or joint appearances with Mom are coming and the stress in the air will be visible. We know when that same "discussion" with Dad about the kids' behavior is coming and he still won't understand. We've tried to win these battles before, and yet here we are again.

Gideon couldn't defeat the Midianites with an army ten, a hundred, or a thousand times bigger than theirs unless his trust was in God to truly fight the fight for him. And God said he didn't need a big army, just a big trust. But God didn't tell him to go empty-handed. He told him to go prepared.

The three hundred men God chose for the battle were all Gideon would need. Our preparation comes not in comrades but in *convictions*, and they must be just as strong. We prepare with our convictions of truth and integrity. We won't lie or cheat to accomplish our goals. We prepare with our convictions of compassion and understanding. We realize everyone else has feelings, too, and proceed with caution. We prepare with our convictions of hope and optimism. Our families grow and change, and we work toward better days when we learn from the past but don't live in it, allowing faith and forgiveness to move us forward.

Gideon didn't tremble when his sizable army was reduced to a focus group because he had moved on to the preparations. "So Gideon sent the rest of the Israelites to their tents but kept the three hundred, who took over the provisions and trumpets of the others" (Judges 7:8).

After we put our trust in God to bring us His best and prepare to do our part, it's time to obey.

◠ OBEDIENCE

You may feel that obedience is a rare commodity in your home. Maybe you and Dad are struggling with kids who face influences out of your control and they balk at the limits and structure you impose. It doesn't matter. A parent's job is to lead as God leads us. His call for our obedience is never punitive, but it's always prescriptive, just like the obedience we seek from those we parent.

It's not our goal to bully kids into submission, but to provide for them a safe and secure home where the parents are in control because, at the risk of sounding cliché, parents know better. You and Dad see beyond the narrow view the kids have and can factor in what they don't know to take better care of them in ways they don't even understand. God does the same for us.

What you allow and don't allow in your home is for the benefit of the entire family and for the peace and protection of everyone involved. Curfews and dress codes, respect and restraint, language and lies—it's all part of the structure that you establish for your home so that life goes more smoothly, goals are accomplished, and characters are made strong.

God's request for our obedience is to the same end. Our lives go much more smoothly when we trust in His bigger view, prepare ourselves, and obey His directives. His and our goals get accomplished when we follow Him, and our character becomes more a reflection of Him as we more closely align with Him. Yes, sometimes we can be an unruly child and balk at what He says and expects, but that's usually because of our shaky trust and unmet preparations. His goal hasn't changed.

If we choose to trust Him, we can surrender this stepfamily to Him, this effort to stepparent the best we can, this day and this hour. And if we trust Him to make the decisions that are best for us, then we can prepare ourselves the best we can for this day and this hour. And if we're prepared, then we can step out in faith to do what He says, to seek no more assurance than that, to act this day and this hour in obedience.

We can hope for a pattern similar to Gideon's in our families. We can help that along with the model of our own *trust*, *preparation*, and *obedience*. No, it won't be quick or painless or without a few missteps, but it's the best plan we have. It worked for Gideon.

Dividing the three hundred men into three companies, he placed trumpets and empty jars in the hands of all of them, with torches inside. "Watch me," he told them. "Follow my lead. When I get to the edge of the camp, do exactly as I do. When I and all who are with me blow our trumpets, then from all around the camp blow yours and shout, 'For the LORD and for Gideon.' "
JUDGES 7:16–18

SOMETIMES WE MESS UP

God's a great teacher. He's patient with us and gives us all the instruction and guidance we need. He presents opportunities to help us grow and then demonstrate everything we've learned. Sometimes we get it right. Sometimes we don't.

Stepmoms are usually operating from a place of pain, and even when we want nothing more than to be good at our jobs, the pain we're struggling with can take over and we respond in ways to protect ourselves. That's not always bad, but sometimes we react too quickly and with a little too much venom. We throw away an opportunity for something good, and the guilt follows. Boy, I know that well.

I can look back now and wonder why I was so hard to get along with all the time. Yes, the control freak in me could argue with you about the reasons for my behavior, but let's just say I could have done better. I could have been more patient, more compassionate, and more understanding.

And now I am, because God was.

◯ STEP STOP

We don't start feeling more comfortable in our stepmom
skin without effort, without trying and failing, and without
knowing intimately what doesn't work. God knows, too,
and He knows what will serve us best not only today in the
rejection of a stepchild, but also tomorrow in the struggle
with the rest of the world.

Every new skill and ability molded into the sometimes
weak or resistant stepmom clay we are is fired to become a
permanent relief map to guide us everywhere else. Look at the
challenges you face. They're not only for you the stepmom but
for you the valued, trusted, and loved disciple with great work
to do. Everything counts.

> *You are forgiving and good, O Lord,*
> *abounding in love to all who call to you.*
> *Hear my prayer, O LORD; listen to my cry for mercy.*
> *In the day of my trouble I will call to you,*
> *for you will answer me.*
> PSALM 86:5–7

There may be no other creature on this earth who needs
God's grace more than a stepmom. I know He's had to use a
couple of ocean-sized helpings on me, but I'm sure He still
has plenty left over. Plus, it's recyclable. So when we meet, I'll
be happy to pass what I've been given on to you. That's how it
works.

When we get this role wrong, God is there. When we have no more patience for ourselves or those around us, He says, "Here, take Mine; let Me show you how it works." When we just don't care anymore and we don't know why, He says, "Here, see how I care; let Me show you how it works." When we're tired of trying to survive in a world we don't know, He says, "Here, I understand everything; let Me show you how it works."

The grace with which He handles our broken hearts becomes the grace that guides our willing hands. He takes our frustration, guilt, and sadness and calms it with His patience, compassion, and understanding—not only to ease our pain, but also to use us as a conduit to others. This is what we learn. And this is how we learn to pass it on to others.

We aren't told that the woman who poured perfume on Jesus' feet said anything. Perhaps she didn't have to. We know the times that no words would come from us if we tried, as we cried in pain on the inside with a cry loud enough to reach the heavens. Jesus knew the woman's pain and heard her silent cry. He responded with grace to match the depth of her need for healing. "Her many sins have been forgiven—for she loved much. But he who has been forgiven little loves little" (Luke 7:47).

We see that our cry to God for forgiveness is never unanswered. Through our own falls and blunders, we hurt much, need much, seek much—and find God's grace at the end of our surrender. The question isn't whether God will respond, but whether we'll ask, and accept, God's love so that we can give it away.

Once we experience it, we know how that grace of forgiveness carries us through our pain and makes us available to help others through theirs. And I know He'll never run out, because the more I give away, the more He gives to me, in every circumstance.

Of course, I need the grace of forgiveness every day, because I'm still a little this side of perfect (yeah, ask my stepkids how far), but He generously supplies the grace of wisdom (if I'll accept it), the grace of calm (if I'll wait for it), and the grace of joy (if I'll allow it). His overflowing grace for me only means more for you. See how it works? Yes, you can do it, too.

Excel in this grace of giving.
2 CORINTHIANS 8:7

Chapter 8

And His truth endures to all generations.
PSALM 100:5 NKJV

⌒ . . .I'M DOING GOD'S WORK HERE!

Making the daily shuttle to football practice? Braiding hair at 6:00 a.m.? Refereeing fights at midnight? Watching your stepkids' mom not show up *again* when she says she will? Listening to your husband's defense of his daughter one more time? Canceling plans and rearranging schedules for the weekend? Doing eighteen loads of laundry, on a good day? Calculating the monthly bills and coming up short? It's just a day in the life of stepmothering, right?

We all have those days, don't we? And through them all, we learn and grow. Sometimes we kick and scream. Oftentimes we cry and worry. And then there's more.

The days of stepmothering when we don't feel like everything's falling apart and our efforts are even appreciated, our presence welcomed, and our love returned—those days do come, too. If you haven't lived any of them yet, you will. Or maybe you're moving along and even overlooking what's already happening. Nothing's falling apart too badly and crises are averted almost with ease. God appreciates your efforts, He welcomes your presence, and He returns your love by the bucketful. And He's preparing your family to do the same. Even if they're not there yet, don't give up. Keep working. . . . God is.

I know it can seem hard to think about all you're doing with a long-range perspective and even a philosophical edge when you're struggling to help your family members get along or even to have a civil conversation with your stepdaughter. But practicing all we've discussed makes it easier. Releasing your life to God's control and doing all you do with Him at the core helps. Not one moment of your day, your role, or your life escapes His attention and profound care. He's vigilant, thorough, and in command of all you see and all you don't. What lies before you isn't the answer to everything you see wrong, painful, or confusing. What lies before you is *your* part in it, *God's work* for you today, right here, right now, where you are. That's all. Go ahead—swing. You can't miss.

> *Stand firm. Let nothing move you. Always give yourselves fully to the work of the Lord, because you know that your labor in the Lord is not in vain.*
> 1 CORINTHIANS 15:58

It's all God's work.

When you read a book to your stepchild, when you make snacks for him and his friends, when you hold your stepdaughter while she cries after her boyfriend breaks up with her—it's all God's work. When you teach your stepkids good manners by example, when you forgive their rejection and continue reaching out to them, when you accept their choices as they grow and support instead of criticize—it's all God's work. When you pray for strength and wisdom, when you give thanks for the little things and trust the big ones to come, when you turn to God when you know you can't turn anywhere else and when you don't want to—it's all God's work.

And we're prepared. God always makes those responsible for the work able to do it. He has worked this way for a long time.

> *"I have given skill to all the craftsmen to make everything*
> *I have commanded you: the Tent of Meeting, the ark of the*
> *Testimony with the atonement cover on it, and all the other*
> *furnishings of the tent. . .and also the woven garments. . .and*
> *the anointing oil and fragrant incense for the Holy Place."*
> EXODUS 31:6–7, 10–11

We can adopt this principle for ourselves—surrendering ourselves to God's plan, trusting Him to prepare us with the skills we need—and receive His instruction, guidance, presence, and passion for the job before us.

Every day in the stepmom role means giving yourself fully to something, and every day something new demands more of you. The distractions, insecurity, and fatigue can take over, push you over a line you drew yourself, and threaten your now and tomorrow. But when we give ourselves fully to *God's work*, anything outside that work will just have to wait.

Sometimes God's work looks a lot like making breakfast. Sometimes it feels like hard-won forgiveness wrenched from our gut like the birthing of a box fan. Sometimes it's a word of kindness or touch of grace where none had ever lived. Always it's about following His lead, doing our best, and leaving the rest to Him. That's God's work in whatever way He has provided for us, and it's enough.

Your part that you see today is enough. It's enough because it's always a beginning. It's a mustard seed when planted in the place God picks.

Jesus compared the kingdom of God to a tiny mustard seed, and we can see our steplives as the wide-open fields of potential they are.

> *"It is like a mustard seed, which is the smallest*
> *seed you plant in the ground. Yet when planted,*
> *it grows and becomes the largest of all garden plants,*
> *with such big branches that the birds of the*
> *air can perch in its shade."*
> MARK 4:31–32

We never know what branches of our steplife will grow strongest. We know some may break or never become tall and high. We can't see that far ahead, but we never give up. Our work may reveal sweet magnolia blossoms atop trees that took a lifetime to grow, but we'll take it. We'll wait and see. Stepmom Cynthia did.

"So where am I now? I have two beautiful step-daughters. Lori always says hello and good-bye. Most of the time she says please and thank you. She generally does her chores within a reasonable time frame. She never ignores me. She doesn't give me a lot of attitude. She generally acts pretty decent. We are still not as close as Mindy and I are.

"Mindy and I hug easily and share girlish conversations. We discuss fashion and trends. We exchange tips on healthy eating. We have a fun time shopping. We groom our pets together and generally have a real mother-and-daughter relationship.

"The blended family is not easy. It takes time to find the right mix of parenting and relating to each other. There are good and bad days, as any family encounters. There are some special challenges with discipline and ex-spouses. However, with God by our side, much prayer and intercession, a supportive spouse, godly counsel, excellent books and resources, much patience, clear communication, boundaries and discipline, and time and energy, I believe that each of us can find our special place in the stepfamily and create 'The Not-So-Perfect Blend.' "

You can grow great things in your steplife garden, too. You can tend and care for the fledgling plants of acceptance, friendship, trust, peace, and joy. With a moment of work here or there, with a seedling still standing in a hard wind, with soil to enrich and till, you can raise a safe and trusting place for your family. Don't doubt any effort. From what looks like little, we can grow much.

◯ SOMETIMES IT'S WORK ON ME

When our boys were young and we had to shuttle them to doctor appointments, school events, and everything in between, I thought I had to know everything. You know how it is: If anyone deviates one millimeter from the carefully prepared schedule, everything must halt while we whip out the slide rule and make adjustments to the flow chart. Don't shake your head—you know how we are.

Well, sitting on the porch one summer day for my allotted thirty-four minutes and mentally checking off the tasks accomplished so far while calculating the anticipated time and materials needed for the remainder of the list, my husband told me he was taking my younger stepson to the dentist that afternoon. Clearly, this was a five-alarm development.

That appointment was news to me, so surely you can understand my mental nosedive into SWAT gear and a snap to attention that would put any Marine to shame. My husband didn't. He had the nerve to be put off by my demand to know why I wasn't told, verbally and in writing, the nanosecond he knew about the appointment. "How does this impact your life?" he asked in a snooty way, looking at me with the look he reserved for our nosy neighbor.

I had an answer. "Well, good grief, I'm in charge, don't you know, and if anything happens without my touch or blessing, then surely the Stepmom Police will descend and I'll be carted off for failure to have control over every molecule within my reach, punishable by a minimum sentence of anger and resentment concurrent with suspicion and pouting for a term of not less than way past bedtime and not more than my unnatural steplife."

That answer was in my head. The one that came out was, "Never mind." I know you understand the escalation of my frustration and the dangerous spin such a trauma could send any self-respecting stepmom into, don't you?

Yes, my husband could have solved this ongoing agony by just telling me everything six months in advance and documenting it in triplicate (a notary's stamp would have been a bonus), but no, he didn't. Sometimes he told me things well in advance, sometimes I had to learn for myself, sometimes I learned from the boys' mom, and sometimes I was the last to know. But as my little mustard plant grew, God worked on me through the control I didn't have or need, helping me to learn to distinguish between the dental visit that truly didn't require congressional approval and wasn't worth suiting up for, and the many things in our life like questionable relationships or school decisions that did require something from me.

And today, after years and years of—arrrrggg—*growing,* I'm way better.

Sometimes "God's work" is working on *us.* In my case, working on me kept Him pretty busy much of the time. I'd like to tell you I've graduated to some level where His constant monitoring isn't necessary. I can't. God does work in mysterious, and constant, ways. Oh, the joy.

◯ THAT CONSTANT WALK WITH GOD

Even with our best intentions and newfound strength, we struggle with our will and way. We need God's constant endurance when ours is failing. Sometimes we don't know what to do even if we have the energy and know-how, when no strategy or direction is clear, but He'll provide it. He'll show us the one thing to do next when we turn to Him for guidance and accept His word. When steptroubles rush in like unharnessed waves and your underwater gear is sparse, throw your net where Jesus says.

> *Early in the morning, Jesus stood on the shore,*
> *but the disciples did not realize that it was Jesus.*
> *He called out to them, "Friends, haven't you any fish?"*
> *"No," they answered. He said, "Throw your net on the*
> *right side of the boat and you will find some." When they*
> *did, they were unable to haul the net in because*
> *of the large number of fish.*
> JOHN 21:4–6

And so it is with us. We can cast our net into waters of the improbable. If your natural response is quick and damaging, consider replacing it with patience and withholding judgment. If you're upset by unmet expectations, consider adjusting them from the ridiculous to the reasonable. If the opportunity comes to dive into the deep end of trust in your stepdaughter or her mom, go ahead and jump in.

Peter and the others didn't find what they expected when they cast their net as Jesus said, but the improbable led to the impossible made possible because Jesus spoke it so. He has no less interest in your fishing. Go ahead. Throw your net where Jesus says.

Approach your stepchild in a different way. Approach his mom in a different way. Put some fun into your daily life and have fun with your stepkids. Set aside some time for your husband and build a stronger marriage. Live your life as if God is in charge.

Jesus doesn't expect us to raise the fish, build the boat, and string the net. He just expects us to do His work one cast at a time.

☽ STEP STOP

One skill we get plenty of practice at is holding back when we're hurt or angry, perhaps because the early days of a stepfamily are especially full of clashes that can leave deep canyons of pain. But when we're ready to form a posse and go after the offending party, we can instead practice that skill by forming a habit of *reverence*, *devotion*, and *surrender*.

Moses asked the Israelites in the desert, after they'd already given in to their fear and abandoned the truth that had brought them that far: "What does the LORD your God ask of you but to fear the LORD your God, to walk in all his ways, to love him, to serve the LORD your God with all your heart and with all your soul, and to observe the LORD's commands and decrees?" (Deuteronomy 10:12–13).

We might ask ourselves the same questions and delight in the answers. What the Lord asks of us, then and now, is a focus on Him: *reverence* for who He is and the love and power made possible because of that, *devotion* to His plan that works to bring us His best and lets us be a part of the best for others, and *surrender* to His timing, methods, practices, and ways because we trust He's smarter than we are.

Our work is our practice every day.

JOY IN CHANGE

Our steplives demand we change. Or maybe God works through us to help us want that change so much that we don't even care *why* anymore; we just appreciate the *how*. God's pursuit of us during these hardest times of our lives and our drop at His knees to receive His breath of grace, compassion, and strength have changed us from a stepmom lost to a disciple found and ready for more.

He has taken the life we couldn't master or control, and in return given us one we don't need to because He already is. The beauty of His plan is new joy we never expected. You know it now.

It's a new mind-set, a new trust you're living, and isn't it wonderful? And addictive? Learning to surrender to God, to leave the control of everything to Him, to do only what He says and let go of the worry and responsibility of what isn't yours—it's a new way to live your role as stepmom and your role as His daughter.

I don't want to give it up. I don't want to abandon this practice even if my steplife troubles go the way of rotary phones. I don't want to go back.

We adapt and change for the better as we live this role, if we'll allow God's hand on us to guide us. We learn new coping skills, tact and diplomacy, empathy and compassion, a new outlook and a new *inlook* at ourselves we wouldn't have gotten otherwise. Some habits and changes we wouldn't want to put back in old wineskins if we could.

"No one sews a patch of unshrunk cloth on an old garment,
for the patch will pull away from the garment, making
the tear worse. Neither do men pour new wine into old wineskins.
If they do, the skins will burst, the wine will run out and the
wineskins will be ruined. No, they pour new wine into
new wineskins, and both are preserved."
MATTHEW 9:16–17

◯ ANOTHER HAT

I promise you'll like this one. I know you feel like a hat rack with all the jobs you already have, but the job I'm talking about here supports all the others, guides you flawlessly, and brings you too much joy to keep to yourself. Paul tells us that we are "Christ's ambassadors, as though God were making his appeal through us" (2 Corinthians 5:20). That responsibility starts here, now.

And what better place than in a family fractured by loss and riddled by bitterness? What better opportunity than with those who love us and those who might not? What better time than when nothing is easy and everything is fragile? What better way than in a role where the potential for so much is so hard to grasp?

Ambassadors go in front, lead and help, deliver information, and connect those they guide with something bigger. That's you and me. That's a stepmom. That's doing

God's work every day in the most important place of all—
home.

When Jesus was resurrected from the grave, the first
people He wanted to see were His disciples, those closest to
Him who would be His mirrors to the world.

So the women hurried away from the tomb, afraid yet filled with joy,
and ran to tell the disciples. Suddenly Jesus met them. "Greetings," he
said. They came to him, clasped his feet and worshiped him.
Then Jesus said to them, "Do not be afraid. Go. . . ."
MATTHEW 28:8–10

And He repeats the pattern with us, because we have a job
to do, too. He finds us, reassures us, and directs us. "Hello,"
He says. "Don't be scared. Here's what I want you to do. . . ."

How is He finishing that point with you today? Do you
see a job right in front of you? It may be so small that it looks
insignificant, but don't you dare believe that. Somebody's
waiting for you.

STEPPING STRONG. . .WHEN JESUS SAYS, "GO!"

With our work comes the grace to do it. We can count on that, and so we proceed in trust and obedience.

> 1. Go in peace. More seeds, more branches is the goal.

> 2. Go in focus. Not my job but yours is all you have to do.

> 3. Go in joy. Today's work is a walk with God; take others along.

> *I will rejoice in the LORD,*
> *I will be joyful in God my Savior.*
> HABAKKUK 3:18

Jesus set an example for His disciples. He made them both students and partners with Him, long ago and far away. And His methods haven't changed. "Anyone who has faith in me will do what I have been doing. He will do even greater things than these" He told them (John 14:12).

Jesus puts a lot of faith in *us*, too, doesn't He? Much of your work is here, in your stepmom-ambassador role, when you're restoring faith in a hurt stepchild, healing a broken relationship, showing God to those who doubt and fear, when you're living a life of courage, gratitude, and joy and inspiring someone else to do the same. That's pretty great work.

Stepmom Stephanie knows the work accepted and done. Her words could be yours, if not now, later. Greater things are coming.

Two children came into my life nearly six years ago.
One was two, the other four. Their parents were no longer
living together. They lived with their dad;
they didn't Have a full-time mom anymore.

I started dating their father and soon felt that our growing
friendship was becoming something more.
The children were shy at first, and so was I.
They didn't know what to think of me, and I didn't know
what to say or do. I only know that I loved
their daddy and that he loved them, too.

It didn't take long for me to fall in love with them,
although it took awhile to gain their trust.
I soon became their mother figure when they had
just about given up.

The more I spent time with them,
the more it broke my heart
that two innocent children's lives could be
torn apart.

I only asked for friendship, but had gotten something more.
In these brief six years as I have watched them grow,
I learned about a special love that I hadn't ever felt before.

Even though these children were not mine,
I knew that I could never love them more.
And I thank God with all my heart for all
that I learned when he was two and she was four.

So the next time you're tempted to throw your hands up in despair, speak words that would peel paint, and ask yourself and anybody else in a four-state radius, "What am I *doing* here?". . .listen.

Listen for the answer in the look of your stepchild, the gratitude you never thought would come, the heart and home you're building one prayer at a time, and you'll know. "I'm doing *God's work* here. And with His grace I'm doing it well."

I can do everything through him who gives me strength.
PHILIPPIANS 4:13

Chapter 9

Unchanging God, Changing Me

⟡ . . .NEVER ALONE, GROWING IN HIS GRACE

Nobody said this role would be easy. We may have thought it for one fleeting, hopeful, delusional second, but we learned the sobering reality soon enough, didn't we?

And we've learned so much more, mostly about ourselves, about how we want to live our lives, where to work and how to change for the better. We've discovered God's indelible touch and unending control on the complexities of our lives. And we can rest. We can release our grasp on every splintered fiber of our families and find our new beginning as we surrender all to God, who guides everything we do.

Our prayers of despair, insecurity, hurt, and anger are replaced by our pledge to take the work we can handle best and leave the rest to God. We can live and deliver our message.

May the words of my mouth and the
meditation of my heart be pleasing in your sight,
O LORD, my Rock and my Redeemer.
PSALM 19:14

That about covers everything, doesn't it? If we can work to please God with our words and thoughts, then we'll be doing what He asks us to do: reflecting Him to those around us, reflecting His grace, love, forgiveness, compassion, joy, and peace. That prayer is our guiding gauge to growing stronger every day, even when we're scared.

Jairus was a synagogue ruler whose young daughter had died. Those with him saw no point in going to Jesus about her.

> *Ignoring what they said, Jesus told the synagogue ruler,*
> *"Don't be afraid; just believe."*
> MARK 5:36

Then the girl lived again. If your stepfamily is dead or wilting, can it be resurrected? Is there any point in going to Jesus? We don't know what the outcome will be, but we certainly know that there is no improvement, no growth when we give up. Our surrender to God puts the future of our families in His hands, but we can do our part—"Don't be afraid; just believe."

Don't be afraid of the facts you're facing now, as depressing or frightening as they are. *Believe* in God's abilities in every situation, in His concern, His presence, His hand on everything you see and everything you don't. Practice reflecting that courage and belief to those around you, because we never know the outcome of our choice to reach out. We never know the impact we'll have on others, but we know the opportunity. It's every day, every moment, in the everyday life of a family trying to grow. It's been played out beautifully in Samara's family.

Samara Tilkens Postuma, a stepmom of two in Minnesota, has been married to her husband, Jeff, for four years. She also has a two-year-old son and a new baby on the way. Her example of grace graces us all.

"The biggest thing that has helped me in my relationship with my stepkids' biological mother is realizing that she is human, too. She is not some shadowy character waiting in the dark plotting ways to make my life difficult. She is someone, like me, doing the best that she can, in the best way she knows how, and it probably won't be perfect, in the same ways I'm not perfect, because we're both human.

"Just like it is easy for stepmoms to be cast in the negative light of evil and dark witches, it is easy to categorize ex-wives and biological moms as these evil, crazy beings, too. When really there doesn't have to be any bad guy; there doesn't have to be the good side and the bad side. Chances are she is a person like you, like me.

"The day I met her, it was sunny outside, and me, being young, in love, and crazy about her children, I couldn't wait to meet her. Why, yes, I'd heard all about her at this point, but this was different. Deep down inside, I wanted her to like me. Because I think that I subconsciously knew that without her support, without her respect, I would never be able to make it in this setup.

"I stood confidently as my future husband introduced me to his ex-wife and reached my hand out to meet hers. She shook my hand, said hello, hugged her kids tight, and got right back in the car, never once removing her sunglasses. That was so not what I was thinking.

"Afterward, I wondered, I analyzed, I and realized over

time that I cannot even imagine what those moments must have felt like for her. Can you imagine being introduced to your ex-husband's new girlfriend? Someone your children like? I sure can't, and realizing this made such a difference to me, because it made her human. Had that been me that sunny day, I don't even like to think of how I would be tempted to act.

"My husband and I were married just two years when we were blessed with our own child, Henry. She brought the kids to see us and the baby hours after he was born, and again, I was stuck by her humanness. Could there be anything harder than those moments? Bringing your children to see your ex-husband and his wife and new child in the hospital? Yet she did, and she did so with grace.

"Having Henry only compounded this idea of humanness between her and me. I realized how much she was giving me. She was in a sense sharing her children with me for half of every week. She could have hated me, she could have said mean things about me, and she could have silently hoped and prayed that I would disappear. But she didn't. She loved her children enough to share them.

"I know that we are blessed to be close. We are blessed to get along, to talk, and to truly try to work together for the kids and ourselves. It is not always sunshine and rainbows; the storm clouds come our way as well. But in the end, the ex-wife in my life is a person, just like me. We will never be perfect. We will never get it all right. Instead, we will make mistakes together and keep on trucking along, knowing that we are all human and we are all doing the best that we can."

Battle-scarred veterans of the steplife chronicles we become; our pine straw walls remain. Like little girls who build houses as they please, we come to know where our powers lie. The world around us may dictate the terrain, but we rake and direct with a vision and a faith in the One who oversees all.

Our power is not over the people in our lives or the circumstances around us. Our power is in our surrender—a paradoxical approach that focuses on raking new walls and building new wings for our family by choice.

We control nothing but ourselves, and we come to rest in that choice, because God says we can. He remains in charge and plans to keep it that way. We realize that control of ourselves is the only full-time job we need, and any assistance He requires from us will fall within that doable description because He knows our limitations well.

We can't fix everything and everyone. We can't blend a family like eye shadow. We *can* keep building, trusting, and releasing the power we have to touch others, the power of a life turned over to God and then back to those we love. Anything is possible.

> *"He performs wonders that cannot be fathomed,*
> *miracles that cannot be counted."*
> JOB 5:9

Father, please help me hold on to You and trust the unchanging love and grace You overflow into my life. Help me know the depth of Your wisdom and compassion and follow Your guidance with courage and conviction. Make clear to me my message and walk with me as I joyfully live and deliver it. Help me remember that You know all my family and I need and You will provide it. I pray to be part of the miracle You're working in my home today, as we start in my heart. Amen.